THIS IS A B
TRANSFO

We all yearn to be free, live a joyous life and reach our highest potential, yet something holds us back. We keep searching for answers outside us in the world of form and yet the Heaven we seek is always within us. It is through grace we take a U-turn within and realize the Self, the source of all love, peace, and joy.

A psychiatrist and mystic, the author has offered a synthesis of key transformative insights from different spiritual traditions, his own spiritual journey, and practical wisdom gleaned from over thirty years of clinical practice.

With practical tips, reflective questions, and simple meditative exercises, you will be able to:

- Dive deep within and gracefully blossom in consciousness like a flower, petal by petal
- Understand the ways of the ego and transcend it by witnessing rather than identifying with it
- Expand in awareness and respond to life with acceptance, kindness, and compassion
- Dissolve pain and suffering through forgiveness and unconditional love for self and others
- Grow in wisdom and maturity through self-reflection
- Learn to live in the Here and Now
- Create a spiritual life that suits your unique temperament and personality
- Manifest abundance in all areas of your life with effortless ease
- Practise the art of conscious healing of body and mind
- Experience peace and harmony within yourself and in your relationships
- Realize that love, peace, and joy is the nature of the Self
- Discover your life purpose and let your light shine

Excerpts from reviewers' comments:

The author's friendliness and personal touch is palpable and that makes it easier to grasp the message. I like the interactive part especially the reflective questions and the awakening exercises. The author has a very rich and varied spiritual exposure.

— Hifzia Bajramovic, M.D., psychiatrist,
faculty member at the University of Ottawa.

What an amazing work. So inspiring, clear and uplifting. The book is filled with grace. You have the ability to synthesize different concepts and truth that have been spoken about for centuries and bring it together in the most natural way. I was really moved with the second chapter on 'my spiritual journey'. The book is full of insights and practical tips for supporting our journey in Self-realization and yet it doesn't sound at all condescending or know it all which is a major achievement given the nature of the book.

— Marie-Sylvie Roy, Ph.D. C. Psych., psychologist and Journey Presenter.

The book is loaded with very useful ideas especially the key point summary at the end of each chapter. I was very touched by the chapter on "perpetual joy is possible."

— Alan D. Reid, Q.C., lawyer and author of
Seeing Law Differently: Views from a Spiritual Path.

Excerpts from reviewers' comments:

The book is a valuable resource for anybody that is awakening. The easy to follow exercises and examples from your own life are very helpful. The chapter on "Forgiveness" — priceless! Many people will pay for these lessons. Your sharing of life experiences is precious! How many people can share such a Journey?

> *— Rolph Fernandes, originally a Franciscan friar for forty-three years, an international lecturer and now serving as an inter-faith minister in the Montreal area.*

I am inspired by the clear possibility for everyone to become the ushers of Heaven and hence co-creating a beautiful world. The book offers many loving, original thoughts as well as a synthesis of timeless wisdom in a simply profound way. The book will be a source of peace and light to the world that seems to be out of control.

> *— Raminder Singh, former international journalist, Canadian Human Rights Commission Officer, and currently a financial advisor.*

Sunder Arora has intertwined intuitive spiritual wisdom with professional psychoanalytical experience as an MD, and presented an inspirational book which is quite easy to follow, and easy to relate to your own life situation.

> *— Surinder J. Singh, the author of* The Power of Raw Thought.

USHERING *in* HEAVEN

A Psychiatrist's Prescription *for* Healing, Joy, and Spiritual Awakening

Sunder S. Arora, M.D.

GSPH

GENERAL STORE PUBLISHING HOUSE
499 O'Brien Road, Box 415
Renfrew, Ontario, Canada K7V 4A6
Telephone 1.613.432.7697 or 1.800.465.6072
www.gsph.com

ISBN 978-1-926962-22-1

Copyright © 2011 Sunder S. Arora

Design and formatting: Magdalene Carson
Printed by Custom Printers of Renfrew Ltd., Renfrew, Ontario
Printed and bound in Canada

Library and Archives Canada Cataloguing in Publication

Cataloguing in Publication data may be obtained from Library and Archives Canada.
Arora, Sunder S.
    Ushering in heaven : a psychiatrist's prescription for healing, joy and spiritual awakening / Sunder S. Arora.
ISBN 978-1-926962-22-1
    1. Spiritual healing. 2. Meditations. 3. Joy. I. Title.
BL624.2.A76 2011   204'.4   C2011-903385-2

The author of this book does not dispense medical advice or prescribe the use of any technique as a form of treatment for any physical, emotional, or medical problem without the advice of a physician, either directly or indirectly. The intent of the author is only to offer information of a general nature to help a seeker in the quest for spiritual and emotional well-being.

In gratitude to my beloved mother,

Ranjit Kaur,

for being an oasis of unconditional love, simplicity, and wisdom.

CONTENTS

A Heartfelt Prayer / *x*

Foreword by Stanislav Grof, M.D. / *xi*

Acknowledgements / *xii*

A Word from the Author / *xiii*

1   Ushering in Heaven / *1*

2   My Spiritual Journey / *13*

3   Awareness / *35*

4   The Dance of Two Selves / *46*

5   How to Awaken / *64*

6   The Eternal Now / *82*

7   Developing Emotional Maturity / *91*

8   Dissolving Pain and Suffering / *99*

9   Learning to Forgive / *108*

10   Conscious Healing / *119*

11   Creating Heaven in Relationships / *130*

12   Effortless Manifestation / *138*

13   Perpetual Joy Is Possible / *148*

14   Being an Usher / *162*

Appendix A: My Transformational Creed / *173*

Mission Statements / *178*

Appendix B: The Transformative Journalling Process / *182*

Spiritual Diary / *186*

Glossary / *188*

Bibliography of Transformative Books / *197*

About the Author / *201*

A HEARTFELT PRAYER

May the truth within this book help you to remember
who you really are and your life's purpose.

May the aspiration flame within you burn brightly,
and may you experience the joy of your Self.

May all aspects of your life be healed and transformed
by this joy and higher consciousness.

May the whole universe be blessed by your awakening.

May all sentient beings, plants, animals,
and the inanimate universe be blessed.

May you be ushers of higher consciousness
and co-create a heaven on Mother Earth.

Om . . . Shanti (peace) . . . Shanti (peace) . . . Shanti (peace) . . .

With Metta (loving kindness)
Sunder S. Arora (Vyasa)

FOREWORD

In the confusing complexity of modern life, psychiatrists and psychotherapists have the difficult task to ease the vast personal suffering of their clients. Connecting with the spiritual source can provide invaluable help in coping with the challenges contemporary humanity is facing. Dr. Sunder Arora, a psychiatrist, interfaith minister, and inspiring spiritual teacher, has written a unique book that can serve as a useful guide for inner life and for the spiritual journey. In the best of traditions, he teaches by sharing spiritual lessons that he has learned, as well as by describing his personal experiences. He discusses the promises and challenges of the spiritual path and puts special emphasis on the importance of forgiveness, gratefulness, and love.

In his book, Dr. Arora expounds on how to expand and elevate one's consciousness through regular spiritual practice. Using his Awakening Practices, insights, and practical tips, he shows how to personalize timeless wisdom and how to bring joy into everyday life. His book is a major gift to all attempting to walk the spiritual path and achieve inner growth.

— Stanislav Grof, M.D., author of *Psychology of the Future*,
The Cosmic Game, *When the Impossible Happens*,
and *The Ultimate Journey*

ACKNOWLEDGEMENTS

I wish to offer my heartfelt gratitude:

To Providence for inspiring me and making me a channel for this work to flow through.

To my parents and ancestors for sowing seeds of spirituality in my life through their love, prayers, role models, and simplicity.

To all the teachers who shared their wisdom so generously and taught me by their example.

To my soulmate and wife, Rupinder, for supporting me in countless ways to make this vision a reality.

To my beautiful children, Sonu and Monu, for their deep love and sharing.

To all my clients and the people who have crossed my path and shared their journey intimately, in the process teaching me many valuable lessons.

To my loyal staff, Claudia, for typing this manuscript and providing logistical support

To staff at General Store Publishing House: Tim Gordon, publisher, for undertaking this project; Jane Karchmar, my editor, for her patience, support, and mindfulness in improving the quality of the manuscript; Magdalene Carson, the art director, for her creative genius; and Alison Roesler, the publicist, for her enthusiasm and dedication.

To the following friends and family members who took time out of their busy schedules to review the manuscript and offer me constructive and invaluable feedback: Dr. Rupinder Arora, Dr. Hifzia Bajramovic, Dr. Sekha Bajramovic, Mr. Rolph Fernandez, Ms. Larissa Gough, Dr. Paul Grof, Dr. Stan Grof, Mrs. Claudia Ramirez, Mr. Alan Reid, Mrs. Barbara Reid, Dr. Marie Sylvie Roy, Mr. Raminder Singh, and Mr. Surinder J. Singh.

A WORD FROM THE AUTHOR

Science tells us that our universe is about 13.8 billion years old. For most of us, it would be very difficult to grasp even the idea of a million years. However, if you take this astronomical time of 13.8 billion years and equate it with a twenty-four-hour scale, it becomes somewhat easier to comprehend. On this scale, zero hours would be the moment of the "Big Bang," and today would mark the end of the twenty-fourth hour. It was about sixteen hours — two-thirds of the total age of the universe — before our sun came into existence. Then it took a few more hours for our solar system and the planets, including Earth, to evolve. The span of human existence is only a blink on this twenty-four-hour time scale. Some people might conclude from this scientific information that our existence is just trivial in the evolution of the universe and therefore feel disheartened. On the contrary, I would invite the reader to consider that we are so very special and such a cherished creation that the universe has taken most of 13.8 billion years to set the stage for our arrival!

Our human existence is precious and an unparalleled opportunity for us to realize who we really are beyond our visible form. It is only through us that consciousness is capable of becoming conscious of itself. The whole manifest universe has been patiently waiting for us to awaken and usher in an era of new consciousness. The biblical prophecy of a new heaven and a new earth is perhaps pointing to this inevitable outcome of our awakening.

This book is an inspired work and a love offering to my world family. I am blessed with both a scientific and a mystical side. I have deliberately chosen to keep things simple and speak from my personal experience rather than burdening the reader with scientific references and the latest research. It has been a privilege to witness the lives of many souls who have crossed my path over the years. To safeguard the privacy of the people whose stories are told in this book, their identifying information has been changed, except when I have the permission from the person to mention his or her name.

To sustain the flow of ideas, the meaning of a foreign word or phrase is generally provided in the same sentence. However, for deeper appreciation of these foreign words, I have added a glossary at the end of the book for easy reference. The books and scriptures that I have found to be transformative in my journey are mentioned in the bibliography. If something in this book challenges your paradigm or triggers you in some way, my request is to just observe the emotional reaction and keep reading. Truth is like rain: it can water the seeds of awakening within you if you are receptive. My suggestion is that you read it with your heart; keep a silent mind rather than letting your intellect create a barrier by indulging in excessive thinking. May your reading of this book be fruitful and transformative.

USHERING IN HEAVEN

Where there is no vision, the people perish.
Proverbs 29:18

The Birth of a Vision

For most of my adult life, I had the inner urge to contribute to my world family through writing and sharing the many insights gleaned from my personal and professional life. But something always held me back. I explained it away by rationalizing that perhaps I had too much on my plate or that I was not disciplined enough or I did not have the proper focus, talent, and patience to get down to the task of actually doing it. It was about eight years ago when I met a book coach, Dr. Serena Williamson, at a service of the Unity Church of Ottawa. Upon invitation, she came to our home and, in chatting with my wife and me, she encouraged us to write a book based on our life experiences and our unique background in science and spirituality. We had been practising physicians for over twenty-five years. Apart from our clinical work, we had also been seekers on a spiritual quest for most of our adult life and recently were ordained as interfaith ministers. Somehow in the conversation the word *"Heaven"* came up and it seemed to activate a dormant seed of a vision in my subconscious mind. This book is a gradual unfolding of that dormant seed of heaven consciousness. Only recently have I become aware of the word *"Heaven"* in our family mission statement; it had been staring at us for the past twenty years.

Later that same year, while strolling with my wife in the market area of downtown Ottawa, we noticed a palm reader's sign in a café window. My wife expressed an innocent desire to have her palm read. Since teenage days, I have had an aversion toward all palmists or fortune tellers. This had to do with an incident that involved my maternal uncle, who claimed to be a palm reader. He pronounced after a cursory glance at my hand that there was not much travel predicted by the lines in my hand, and that I would never see an ocean. It felt like a death sentence to an eighteen-year-old with hopes and dreams of travelling, studying abroad, and seeing the world. Since his reading turned out to be completely incorrect, I decided to believe in the notion that I am the master of my destiny. I consequently tended to avoid psychics and palm readers.

Despite my strong conviction of self-determination and my aversion toward palmists, I found myself influenced by my wife's childlike curiosity and allowed the palm reader to inspect my hand as well. She referred to a book already written by me on the astral level that was awaiting physical expression. This prediction echoed a similar statement made by another psychic whom I had encountered earlier that year at a New Age show. I even remembered having had a vivid dream about it a few years previously. It felt as though the universe was gently nudging me to get on with the task of actually writing this book.

Attending a book launch and listening to the stories of young authors is what finally inspired me to get on with it. I had been postponing writing because I saw it as a distraction from the other pursuits that really mattered to me, such as my spiritual growth. During the process of contemplation, it dawned on me that sharing my journey could become my spiritual practice and would be an expression of deep gratitude to the universe for bestowing me with countless blessings.

So, in the summer of 2003, while exploring the Canadian Rockies, I made my first attempt to start the book and even managed to complete a chapter on Awareness, although with much struggle. It was difficult to maintain the momentum when faced with the demands of a very busy professional and personal life. The final vision of the book was still vague and somewhat unclear. For a while, it felt as though I was staring at a partially cut raw diamond, not knowing where to chisel next.

Somehow the universe kept reminding me of "Heaven." While meditating at our cottage on a glorious fall day during that same year, I was stunned by an unusual awareness of the common words *home* and *hope*. I felt shivers down my spine as the words revealed their acronymic meaning to me. "Home" seemed like an appropriate acronym for "Heaven on Mother Earth," whereas "hope" stood for "Healing of Planet Earth."

Later on that same year, just before Christmas, the word *Heaven* emerged again. This time it was in the context of a life purpose workshop that I happened to attend. I found myself writing the following life purpose statement: "*To experience Heaven within at every moment and to co-create Heaven on Earth.*" This life purpose statement has since become a driving force in my life. You could even say that I have been pregnant with this thought of *ushering in Heaven* for quite some time, and it was about time to deliver or face the consequences of an overdue pregnancy.

My midwife happened to be the Buddhist Lama Tenzin, to whom I had the privilege of listening during Christmas of 2003 at the Sivananda Yoga Ashram on Paradise Island, Bahamas. He created an exquisitely beautiful Mandala of Compassion. A mandala is a concentric design or a pattern that has spiritual and ritual significance in Hinduism and Buddhism. (Someone has already put a short video of his work on YouTube.) In his talk, Lama Tenzin described his inner prayerful process as he was mindfully creating the mandala with coloured sand.

His talk offered me the vital insight that I needed to consider the process of writing this book as similar to a sacred *puja* (worship) instead of an ego-driven task that I had to struggle through. I felt an inner thrill, and within a short span of a couple of hours, the entire outline as well as a title of the book manifested like a divine mandala. The yoga ashram provided me an enriched, high-vibrational environment in which I was able to stay connected to the source of this inspiration. I literally dictated nine chapters of the book in ten days. I would go for a walk on the beach and come back with a note pad full of ideas, feeling enthused and ready to dictate. Writing or typing was not an option, since ideas were pouring out faster than I could jot them down. As soon one chapter was completed, the ideas for the next chapter would start channelling through me. It was an astounding process of birthing a book that seemed to have a life of its own. I just needed to relax, surrender to the source, trust the process, and get out of the way.

In hindsight, it is obvious to me now why writing this book was not possible in the past: my ego was still running the show, and I had not surrendered enough to the spirit to let it use me fully as an instrument. I discovered that my little ego had a million excuses, whereas the spirit had none. "Little Me," another name for my ego, still wonders, who am I to speak of ushering in Heaven? Yet when I listen to whispers of the spirit in silent stillness, it is ever so clear to me that I am a child of God — and who am I to judge how my Creator wants to use me as an instrument?

Even though the initial draft of most of the book was dictated in ten days, it still took seven more years before it was ready for publication. It is as though the baby was born but needed a few more years of love and nurturing before it would be ready for the school of life. Most important, Little Me needed to allow the Higher Self to take over more of my life. I also needed to live and demonstrate the transformative power of the wisdom contained in this book.

By now, you may be wondering, what do I mean by *Heaven?* And where is it? Here I am going to rely on the ancient tradition of passing on the wisdom through stories. Allow the innocence and receptivity within to come forth as you read these stories.

> Once upon a time, there was a brave warrior who had fought many battles and survived them. Now that he was getting old in years, he found himself reflecting on his life and wondering about heaven and hell. He consulted many learned people in his area, but no one could offer him a satisfactory response. It was suggested that he seek counsel from a wise hermit who lived alone in a cottage on top of the mountain. The hermit's cottage was in a rather secluded place, and the warrior had to climb a very steep and treacherous trail to get there. Upon arrival, he found the hermit sitting in a silent meditative pose.
>
> Not wishing to disturb him, the warrior waited for a while before asking his question: "Could you please tell me about heaven and hell?"
>
> The hermit remained motionless, as though he had not heard the question. The warrior decided to repeat his question a second time, and once again there was no response. Even after several repetitions of the question, there was still no reply from the hermit. The warrior felt insulted, and anger flared up within him like a raging fire. Without much thought, he took out his sword to strike at the hermit.

Just as the sword was an inch from the hermit's neck, the hermit opened his eyes and said, "This is hell."

The warrior was stunned. He felt extremely ashamed of his behaviour and bowed down in sincere apology, touching the hermit's feet with tears in his eyes. The hermit lovingly lifted the warrior's head and, gazing gently into his eyes, said in a sweet voice, "My son, this is Heaven."

The second story is about a man who in his dream had died and found the angel of death standing by his side. Being inquisitive by nature, he asked the angel to show him heaven and hell before it was decided where he would go. The angel agreed and took him into an elevator. As the doors opened, he found himself in a dining room with a large table and a scrumptious feast spread out on the table. The angel described this place as "hell." This really puzzled the man until a bell rang, and he saw the double doors open and a crowd of people come in with long spatulas fixed to their arms, preventing them from bending their arms. They all seemed very hungry and looked rather emaciated. Very soon, the dining room turned into bedlam, and pandemonium broke out as these hungry, emaciated people were trying to eat food with the long, spatula-like spoons without being able to bend their elbows. There was much pushing and shoving, and the food was flying in the air and littering the floor. As a result, none of them got any nourishment, and the whole room was in disarray. The bell rang again, and they all departed, feeling more frustrated, hungrier, and angrier than they were when they came in. The man thought this must surely be hell.

The man then turned to the angel and requested to be shown heaven. In a flash, the scene changed and it seemed like they were in an identical room with the same layout of a delicious feast in front of them. "This is heaven," said the angel. The man thought that perhaps the angel was mistaken. Once again, the bell rang, the double doors opened, and another large crowd of people came in. They also had the same long, spatula-like spoons attached to their arms but they did not look emaciated. Instead, they seemed well-nourished and of cheerful disposition.

Very gently and lovingly, they sat on the chairs, said grace, and started to feed each other across the table with their spoons.

There was much laughter and pleasant conversation during the meal. By the time the bell rang again, they were all satiated and expressed their love and gratitude to each other as they left the dining room joyously. So, thought the man, this surely is Heaven.

I hope by now you can appreciate that *heaven* is a *state of consciousness* and not a place somewhere in the sky. It is a non-judgmental and expansive consciousness of love, peace, joy, and creativity. It feels like being on-line with the Source — another way to refer to God. Through my interfaith and inter-spiritual journey, it is very obvious to me that the *heaven consciousness* is no different than what we often refer to as higher consciousness, Christ consciousness, Krishna consciousness, or Buddha nature. A helpful metaphor is that of water. Once you have tasted it, no matter by what name it is called in different parts of the world, you can always recognize it and quench your thirst.

Whether we are aware of it or not, we are always seeking this heaven consciousness. As a psychiatrist, it is very evident to me that we all have very similar yearnings at a deeper level, even though on the surface we may identify ourselves with a different race or religion or a certain socioeconomic group. My clients are primarily seeking relief from a medical or psychiatric condition. In addition to that, they may be in search of a new relationship, a better job, improved health and wellness, financial success, name, or fame. When I sense that they are ready to get in touch with their deepest yearnings, I usually ask them some variation on the question: *"So what do you really want?"*

It is truly amazing to discover how similar people are at the level of their deepest yearnings. They may use different words, but ultimately everybody yearns for peace, joy, freedom, abundance, love, a sense of being here for a purpose, security, feeling alive, self-worth, and fulfillment. One may call it "peace of mind," while another person may refer to this as "serenity." Some may use a word such as "abundance," while another may describe it as "prosperity." These qualities that we all yearn for are intangible, formless, and cannot be measured in a lab and are therefore very subjective. *But they must have some basis in reality, since we spend our whole life seeking them.* One of Rumi's poems puts this seeking in proper perspective.

Friends, you seek the formless,
You are really seeking the Divine
And don't even know it

These formless qualities are an aspect of the Divine. They have also been referred to as "fruit of the spirit" in the Bible. *"But the fruit of the spirit is love; joy, peace, patience, kindness, goodness, faithfulness"* (Galatians 5:22). So in a way, at the level of our yearnings we are all seeking the Divine, even though we may describe ourselves as atheists.

While interviewing a teenager, I asked him, "What are your views on God?"

Very confidently he replied, "I do not believe in God. I am very scientific; I believe in the Big Bang theory."

Then, after some further exploration, I asked him one of my transcendental questions: "So what is the purpose of your life?"

And again without a moment's hesitation, he answered, "I seek joy and higher levels of joy."

I just smiled and recalled the profound wisdom in Rumi's poem. These formless qualities are actually aspects of our *Being*, which is always one with the Source. They could also be seen as an expression of heaven consciousness.

Even though we yearn for peace, love, joy, and freedom, yet we usually seek them outwardly in worldly pursuits in a new job, a new relationship, financial success, or whatever our quest may be. We are no different than the deer in the jungles of India that grows musk in its belly but smells it outside. The deer gets exhausted running from bush to bush looking for this enchanting fragrance but never finds it, since it is always within him. Like the deer, far too many people have already suffered enough and are starting to question the effectiveness of this materially directed, seeking paradigm of *Have/Do/Be* that we are all born into. Even if one temporarily succeeds, there is such a high emotional, relational, and health cost that it seems like a very hollow accomplishment. Yet we still find ourselves driven by this paradigm. We are taught that in order to be happy and experience fulfillment, we need to *Have* a certain degree of educational, financial, and worldly success. Then we can *Do* all the things we want and, in the end, it is to be hoped that we will *Be* happy and fulfilled.

It sounds very reasonable but it does not work. This paradigm is as inaccurate as saying that the earth is flat. I see the casualties of this *Have/Do/Be* paradigm in the lives of celebrities or people who are "successful" or "have made it" in the eyes of the world.

> Christopher, who is a middle-aged gentleman, is extremely successful from a worldly perspective but he is severely depressed, and all his family relationships are in turmoil. He does not have patience for psychotherapy. All his money can buy him is antidepressants — but not peace of mind, harmony in human relationships, or the state of well-being that he so desperately wants. It has been painful for him to maintain a façade of being very successful, since he could not let down the people who look up to him. I vividly recall his asking me in desperation, "Is that all there is to success?"

When I hear a comment like that, I know that the person has suffered enough and may be ready for awakening. Sooner or later, we all need to realize that the *Kingdom of Heaven* we have been searching for is not outside us but is always within us.

The paradigm that is closer to this spiritual truth is that of *Be/Do/Have*, which is completely opposite to that of the worldly paradigm. You start out by connecting with the divine self (*Being*) within you in silent stillness. From that oneness with the *Being*, you will receive inspiration to take a certain action or pursue a particular profession or choose a direction that will be in alignment with the highest evolutionary impulse of the universe. And as you pursue your passions that are inspired by this deeper wisdom, there will be a different quality to your consciousness. You will be mindful, relaxed, and joyful, rather than expressing the usual ego-based consciousness of stress, frustration, and striving. With this joyful and relaxed consciousness, you have already succeeded, and all your material needs are more than likely to be taken care of abundantly by the benevolent Universe. Most important, you are enjoying your journey *right now* rather than waiting for happiness or fulfillment in some distant future. It is this paradigm that leads to ethical, enlightened, and ecologically friendly businesses, and allows the individuals to truly live out their life purpose. The good news is: There are some indications of positive changes in our society.

Since moving to Canada about thirty-four years ago, I have noticed a definite growth of spiritual consciousness among people all over the world, even though outwardly they may have turned away from organized religion. Even tragedies such as 9/11 have in some way forced us to look within and awaken. When I first wanted to introduce spirituality to the psychiatric department of my university, I was advised by well-meaning colleagues that I should only use words such as stress management. Now, several years later, the same department is spearheading international conferences on spirituality and mental health. The fact that Oprah and Eckhart Tolle have taught a series of spiritual classes on the Internet is a sign that there is a mass-scale awakening happening. Since starting work on this book, I have been invited to give talks on spirituality and mental health sponsored by pharmaceutical companies, which is rather interesting. It is like McDonald's starting to make veggie burgers! These are definite indications that we are living in a very transformative time.

With 2012 around the corner, some people are predicting this to be the end of the world, according to the Mayan calendar. Similar prophesies of Nostradamus and many traditions are suggesting an unusual galactic alignment that happens only once in 26,000 years. The current economic, political, and ecological crisis could make anybody wonder about the fate of humanity. My intuition is that humanity will survive as more and more people will consciously awaken and become ushers of heaven consciousness during these tumultuous times. I envision the dawn of a new era for humanity where the forces of light are finally victorious over forces of darkness; and those souls who are vibrationally ready will act as frequency holders to sustain this grid of higher consciousness.

How a larva transforms into a butterfly has a lot to teach us about what is happening to humanity. Apparently, in the initial stages, the larva consumes a lot of food and can barely struggle to move around. That is no different than the current consumer state of humanity struggling with the uncontrolled proliferation of material stuff. While the larva is struggling, within its body a group of cells referred to as *imaginal cells* are starting to come together in clusters. These cells hold a different reality for the larva. It is as though they are visualizing a butterfly that can fly, have a navigation system, and be a fast metabolizer — having almost nothing in common with the current state of the larva. One day, when a critical mass of these cells is achieved, a gene gets activated, and there occurs a quantum transformation of a larva into a butterfly. Apparently it is the same gene that runs our heart. Similarly, while the world is going through chaos, there are groups of people awakening and coming together through all kinds of networking, and a critical mass is fast approaching. These awakening souls are like imaginal cells in the larval body of humanity. They are holding a vision of a new earth and the dawn of an era of higher consciousness. Transformation could happen as quickly as the coming down of the Berlin wall or the dismantling of the USSR.

I often imagine this world as a giant popcorn maker. In the beginning, the process is slow and only a few kernels pop up, but eventually it speeds up until most kernels pop. Similarly, there has been a handful of realized masters for a long time, and now this wave of awakening is finally reaching a critical mass. In my clinical work, I am noticing an ever-growing number of people who are interested in spirituality. Some of them are even having experiences of spontaneous spiritual openings, or so-called spiritual emergence. In the coming three to five years, we may see many more people spontaneously awakening.

Since our true nature is infinite and eternal, nothing less than the Kingdom of Heaven would satisfy us. *In a way, the purpose of our existence is to awaken to our divine nature and usher Heaven into our lives and the lives of others.* It may be in the form of a book, a song, a painting, a beautiful garden, a social reform, raising beautiful children, or wherever our talents lie. Or we may simply emanate peace, love, and joy and be a lighthouse unto others and remove darkness by our mere presence.

During one of my many spiritual retreats at a yoga ashram, I had the privilege of conversing with many people from different walks of life. They all had a yearning to contribute to the world and leave a positive legacy in their chosen field. My sense is that as we awaken, it is natural for us to be become ushers of heaven. We become a conduit or a channel for heaven consciousness to illuminate the world we live in. That is the way the universe seems to be evolving. The question is: Are you ready and willing to join this transformative process consciously? Or will you drag your feet in resistance?

The life of fulfillment that we all want is possible only if we are willing to awaken and transform our lower ego nature in the light of awareness. This book is an invitation to those who read it and, in a way, to all the members of my human family, to embrace this unique opportunity and align themselves with the highest purpose of their existence. If you have been preparing gradually through some spiritual practice, the birthing process of spiritual transformation can be very gentle and effortless, like a bud opening into a flower. You may not have to do anything differently or change your life in any way. All that may be required is a shift in perception and some mindfulness in how you do things. An embryo does not struggle to become a fully developed baby. As the scriptures tell us, we are all made in the image of God. My spiritual teacher would even say that we are tomorrow's gods in embryo form and our awakening is inevitable.

Key Insights

1. We all have within us a dormant memory of Heaven and we are all yearning to go back home.

2. Heaven is not a place but a consciousness; the Kingdom of Heaven is within us.

3. We are all living our lives in a dark field of mind-body conditioning. We desperately need the light of consciousness.

4. Being in touch with your divine purpose does not require you to drastically change your life. It simply may be an internal shift in perception and in the way you do things.

5. An usher is consciously in touch with the evolutionary impulse of the universe.

Questions to Reflect On

1. How is my relationship with the universe/Source/God?

2. What do I really want for my life? What would truly fulfill me?

3. What does the universe want from me? Is my life filled with purpose?

Awakening Practice (Be Here Now)

Just be fully present to your surroundings, no matter where you are now. Look around you. Pay attention to all the objects around you without naming them. Take your time; no rush. Now be aware of the spaces between the objects. Now close your eyes and pay attention to the various sounds within the body and around you without judging them. Now notice any silence between the sounds. Now pay attention to the sense of touch or a gentle movement of air as it caresses your skin. Observe any taste in your mouth. Notice if there is any smell in the room. No judgments; if you have a judgmental thought, let it go and don't judge yourself for that. Now bring all of the senses together and be aware of the fact that you are aware. Observe the aliveness in your body. Just be with this experience for as long as you like. You can do this exercise anywhere.

2

MY SPIRITUAL JOURNEY

*We don't receive wisdom; we must discover it
for ourselves after a journey that no one can take
for us or spare us.*
Marcel Proust

The world-famous Golden Temple, surrounded by a pond of sacred water, is at the heart of the city of Amritsar. The word *Amritsar* means "pond of divine nectar." This holy city can be compared to Jerusalem in its religious significance to Sikh pilgrims from all over the world. It was in this holy and dynamic city that I had the privilege of being born in free India, only a few years after her independence in 1947. The city is in the northern Indian state of Punjab and is often referred to as the "breadbasket" of India, due to its fertile soil and advancement in agriculture. Amritsar is a mere eighteen kilometres from the Pakistan border and has miraculously survived many wars, riots, and threats of invasion.

My parents were moderate Sikhs and they had a prayer room strategically located in the centre of the house, a tradition that I have come to observe in my family life with the support of my wife, who shares a background similar to mine. As I reflect on my formative years, I can still recall my father chanting the scriptures from the holy book *Sri Guru Granth Sahib*. This was his morning routine after his bath and always before breakfast. These are the only times I ever recall my father singing. Otherwise, he was a very serious and practical person and rarely ever listened to music or hummed a melody. He had a strong, childlike faith in our family guru, whom he often referred to as Maharaj Ji (the great one). Apparently, when I was born, my father biked over sixteen miles on rough country roads to visit Maharaj Ji and to inform him of my birth.

This family guru bestowed upon me my current name, Sunder, and also chose names for my older brothers, Mohan and Sohan. All these names refer to a different aspect of the divine. *Sunder* means "beautiful." God is described in the Hindu scriptures as *Satyam Shivam Sundaram*, meaning, "Truth is God and God is beautiful." For a long time, I had mixed feelings about my name, since it is a rather uncommon name among Sikhs and not a very trendy name among the Hindus, either. But over time, I have come to appreciate it as my good fortune and a rare spiritual blessing of an enlightened sage. The acceptance of my name happened after immigration to Canada. Most of the people I interacted with in the West had either a neutral or a curious response to my name. I am certain that my residency training in psychiatry, four years on the couch in personal psychoanalysis with two analysts, and personal growth contributed to this growing sense of self-acceptance and internal freedom.

My mother, who was all heart and of devotional temperament, would often wake up early in the morning and prepare the prayer room for meditation and scripture reading. She would routinely visit the Golden Temple in the early hours while we were all still asleep. One of my fondest memories of her is greeting her with a big hug as she came through the wooden double doors of our family home after her morning visit to the temple. I can still vividly sense the soft touch of her cotton *saree* and the peaceful vibrations that emanated from her being. She would usually bring home *prasad,* a blessed food from the temple, and I always looked forward to it. She was not formally educated but was very wise and pure at heart. My mother, whom we all lovingly called Bibi Ji, was astute — like a musician who could play music by ear without any training in reading the notes. She had natural, innate wisdom. She consciously prayed for me while carrying me in her womb. From somewhere, she had heard that a mother's prayers do have a profound impact on the baby's consciousness in the womb. Throughout my life, I have always felt her silent prayers sheltering me from dangers like an invisible shield and giving me the confidence when faced with a challenge or a difficult life situation. I often wonder about these incredible blessings and their impact on my spiritual unfoldment.

Many years later in Canada, while watching the *Hour of Power* on TV by Dr. Robert Schuller, I became aware of the profound instant and long-term effects of mothers' prayer. On this particular show, Dr. Schuller was interviewing former Russian president Mikhail Gorbachev. He was expressing deep gratitude to him for permitting an evangelist to be on Russian television during prime time. Gorbachev claimed to be an atheist, but Dr Schuller did not seem to accept his declaration. During that interview, President Gorbachev confessed that his mother often prayed for him, and as a child he grew up with religious icons in his home along with pictures of Lenin. Dr. Schuller made a remark that mothers' sincere prayers are like an ever-growing tree, and Gorbachev had undeniably been blessed by her prayers without his awareness. The late Sri Chinmoy, a New York-based spiritual master and one of my mentors, also had a similar perception of President Gorbachev as quite a spiritual person. Sri Chinmoy became friends with President Gorbachev and his family and dedicated songs and books to acknowledge his spiritual height.

Even now, my eyes well up with tears of gratitude as I acknowledge my mother for planting a prayer tree to watch over my earth walk while I was still resting in a peaceful slumber in her womb. Talk about spiritual insurance — she definitely knew that

"prayer is the most potent action in the universe."

One of my cherished memories of Amritsar was that of sleeping on the flat rooftop in the hot summer months. Every evening, one of us children would cool down the floor of the flat rooftop, rendered unbearably hot by the day's intense heat, by washing it down with several buckets of water. The only way of getting the water up to the top floor was through an old-fashioned hand pump, and it was quite an aerobic exercise to pump up several buckets of water. Once the roof cooled down, then we would make the beds. The beds were actually cots, but far more comfortable than all the expensive mattresses I have tried so far. At night, the canopy of stars above was so mesmerizing that I would often not know just when I fell into a deep, blissful sleep.

I was often woken up in the early hours of the morning, at around four a.m., by the live chanting of hymns from the Golden Temple, the shining dome of which was visible from our rooftop. I did not wear a wristwatch or use a bedside clock but I could accurately tell time by looking at the constellation of stars in the sky. The local Hindu temple (*Durgyana Mandhir*), too, would play recordings of their sacred songs (*bhajans*), to make sure that they also contributed to the collective spiritual vibrations. It was an established morning ritual, and nobody called the police to complain that the local temples were interfering with their sleep. For me the most delightful sleep was from four a.m. to six a.m., while hearing these chants subliminally. They even had a special song at six a.m., in which Lord Krishna's mother is saying to him, "Wake up, wake up, oh Krishna," and that used to be my morning alarm clock. Often the sunrise would lend a hand as well, since it would be virtually impossible to stay asleep when the warm, bright rays of the morning sun were shining on my face.

In the winter months, we would sleep indoors, and the chanting from the temples was barely audible from inside the house, especially with doors and windows bolted shut to keep the thieves out and to keep the house warm, since there was no central heating in those days. Once a year during the winter months, we would have a visiting *sadhu* (a wandering monk), who would start pacing up and down our street in the early hours of the morning chanting God's name. I can still hear his melodious, deep, resonant and comforting voice as I recall those times when I would be lying in bed, all warm and cuddled up under a heavy quilt, and he would be out there in bitter cold weather doing his morning rounds. The early morning hours are considered to be a very auspicious time for spiritual practice. They are referred to as "Time of the Gods," or *Brahma Muhurta*. It is said that a little spiritual practice at that time often yields a bumper harvest, and that is why most ashrams and temples in India have early morning services. The visiting *sadhu*'s morning penance would go on for a month or so. And then finally all the people in our street would feel enough guilt or gratitude to raise some money to finance the *sadhu*'s few basic demands for food, a blanket, and some travel money for his next pilgrimage. This was a yearly event. What a simple and yet spiritually profound life it was, whereby seeds of spirituality were subliminally planted in your subconscious while you were asleep!

I now know without a shadow of a doubt that it is these seeds and blessings (*samskaras*) that later on blossomed into my spiritual quest. All the challenges in my adult life nudged me to awaken instead of escaping by turning to alcohol or one of many self-destructive addictions that can often manifest if there are no *samskaric* seeds of awakening in the subconscious. I see this repeatedly in my clinical practice: not everybody awakens as a result of suffering unless there are already some seeds of spirituality in the consciousness.

In our neighbourhood there lived a class of workers who were often referred to as *Barpunjhas*. They would labour all day in front of the fire, roasting chickpeas and peanuts or making rice cakes and a wide variety of local snack foods. Their skin tone was unusually dark, probably because of all the smoke and the sun that they were exposed to. Once a week, they would have an all-night chanting of spiritual hymns (*Jagrata*). The melodies of these hymns were based on popular songs from the Bollywood movies. Their all-night chanting was a source of considerable distress to me, especially before an important examination, as it would interfere with my ability to concentrate on my studies. People in India are generally very tolerant of these neighbourly activities, and no one complains to authorities about the noise pollution. In order to cope with these distractions, I would go to bed very early, at around nine p.m., and wake up at four a.m., when the neighbourhood chanters would be silent, so that I could finally study in peace. I am eternally grateful to my mother for ensuring that I was not only awake but out of bed and sitting in front of my study table. To help me stay awake and concentrate, she would make me a thermos full of hot tea, which I would sip while studying.

We lived in an extended family system, and it was an example of interfaith harmony. My paternal grandmother worshipped Hindu idols on her personal prayer altar, while my parents had the Sikh scriptures in the prayer room. My paternal grandmother was respectfully addressed as Dadi Ji, but her actual name was Ganga Devi, named after the holy River Ganges. She came from a Hindu family and was married to my grandfather when they were both still children, a tradition that is no longer practised. My paternal grandfather, *Sardar* Atma Singh, was born and raised in a Sikh family and was known for his generosity and service to the community through many philanthropic activities. Interfaith marriages were much more acceptable in those days. Apparently, theirs was a period of Hindu-Sikh harmony when many a Hindu would take pride in having their first-born raised as a Sikh.

Saintly people would often visit our home, usually at the request of my paternal grandmother. I can still recall a few of the teachings of these saintly people, since I would be playing around or curiously watching their interaction with my grandmother. Grandma complained a lot about her asthma. Once I recall a saintly person telling her in a kind voice, "Oh, Mother, instead of complaining a lot about your illness, why don't you let your suffering remind you of God?"

Before a marriage ceremony or any kind of special family function, there were usually a couple of days of continuous chanting of the scriptures (*Akhand Path*) in the prayer room to invoke the divine presence, and in the process, purify the house and seek blessings for the event.

My parents sent me to a traditional Hindu school because of its academic record and were not at all concerned about my being exposed to Hindu gods and goddesses and the Vedic rituals of sacred fire (*yagna*) that were regularly held in my school. Our headmaster (principal), Mr. Dev Raj, was known for his high moral values and strict discipline. He would frequently invite some visiting monks (*swamis*) and saintly people from different traditions to address the student gatherings and impress upon our receptive minds the importance of ethical living and the need for spiritual discipline as a foundation for all worldly pursuits.

Our mornings in the school would start with an assembly in the main grounds, with the singing of spiritual hymns. There were only motivational and spiritual quotations on the school walls, and no graffiti anywhere, since cleanliness was valued and considered to be a prerequisite to godliness. The seeds of spirituality were all-pervasive, and I am grateful for all those silent blessings that later on fuelled my spiritual quest. It is this omnipresent spiritual theme in everyday life that makes India a lighthouse of spiritual wisdom.

One summer, I borrowed from the school library the *Ramayana* and the *Mahabharata*, two spiritual epics of Hinduism, each a thousand pages long. I spent the hot summer afternoons in the cool comfort of our prayer room immersed in these epics for hours instead of taking a siesta. Fortunately, the television had not yet made it to our neighbourhood; otherwise I wonder how I would have spent my summer afternoons. During my school year my favourite goddess (*Ishta Devi*) for inspiration was *Saraswati*, who bestows wisdom and creativity.

As a young teenager, I even explored hypnosis and psychology through self-study of books belonging to my older siblings. This hobby of trying to understand the human psyche later on became a profession for me. My thinking was also broadened by the open-minded writings of Sardar Gurbux Singh, a foreign returned engineer who followed his calling and became a writer and a social reformer. His books were not allowed in our home, since my father felt threatened by Singh's revolutionary thinking that challenged his conservative values and way of life. However, my older brother, Mohan Vir Ji, would secretly share his books and discuss his teachings with me. In many ways, he fulfilled the role of a surrogate father and educated me about sex, literature, Punjabi theatre, and spirituality. While my older brother taught me about the finer things of life, my middle brother, Sohan Vir Ji, modelled for me a very practical and dynamic approach to life. My older sister, whom I affectionately called Didi, was a role model of gentleness, patience, and tolerance. So, being the youngest in the family, I had the best of role models in my older siblings.

My evening strolls, usually after dinner, would invariably take me to the Golden Temple, where I would not only meet my friends and relatives but often encounter foreign tourists. Since I could speak some English, I would deliberately engage them in a conversation and in the process not only get to know them but also act as their unofficial tour guide. They were usually grateful for being able to converse with a local and also receive some helpful tips. Looking back, I wonder how much those conversations contributed to my burning desire to travel abroad for higher education; and also endowed me with the courage to connect with people irrespective of their race or language.

The choice of career was rather a simple decision for me. My middle brother had already staked out the engineering profession, and my older brother was working with my father in his textile business, while struggling to be independent by starting another business on the side. For me, the logical choice was between medicine, working with my father, or doing an arts program (in contrast to the ten thousand career choices young people are faced with these days). As a child, I was very influenced by our family physician, Dr. Bodh Raj, for his serene, reassuring, and confident personality. The other professional who impacted my career choice happened to be my parents' dentist. Interestingly, his name was Dr. Bodh Raj as well, and he had studied in the United States before setting up his practice in Amritsar. I can still bring to mind my visits to his clinic when my mother was getting some dental work done. He would be working on my mother's teeth and at the same time chatting with me and even advising me that I should study and become a professional and go abroad for higher education. I must have been ten or twelve years old and I looked forward to those visits, especially the engaging conversation with the dentist and getting candies at the end of every visit. Now looking back, I find it a bit amusing that as a dentist he would give out candies to me while he would warn against it to all his adult patients. So when the time came for me to choose a career path, which is often done very early in the high school system in India, I chose the medicine track and have never regretted it.

My father had different plans for me. He wanted me to take over his textile business, since my older brother by now had branched off into the oil business. My desire to pursue medicine had a life of its own. It was firm and unyielding and it gave me a sense of quiet inner strength and confidence. As a teenager in an Indian culture where a father's wishes are honoured without question, I could not openly rebel against him. Instead I channelled all of my emotional energies into my studies. I still remember the day when I won the national scholarship. Mohan Vir Ji, my older brother, had gone for a morning walk and came back home quite excited, holding in his hand a rolled copy of a local Punjabi newspaper. He was very proud to announce to the neighbours and to the extended family that his younger brother's name was published in the top fifty out of 10,000 candidates who appeared for the higher secondary exam that year. That meant that I would be entitled to a substantial scholarship if I continued my higher education, and there would be little or no financial dependence on my father, who controlled the family purse. My father in the end yielded to the mounting pressure on him and allowed me to continue my medical studies (and also, being a businessman, he did not want the scholarship to go to waste).

I worked hard during the premedical course, although just before the final exam, I contracted typhoid fever. My resolve was so clear that nothing was going to deflect me. Even a very high fever did not stop me from showing up for my premed exams. I was even unable to review my notes prior to the exam, and my middle brother, Sohan Vir Ji, helped me by reading aloud my notes to me while I was lying in bed delirious with fever. It seems that even the

Universe gives in when you hold back nothing and give all of yourself to anything that you sincerely desire. After the premed exams, I was in bed for two months recovering from the weakness caused by the long-drawn-out fever.

All that suffering seemed like a trivial price to pay for the reward of having my dream come true when I received the admission notice to the Amritsar medical college. By now, my father had reluctantly accepted my career choice as well and even assisted me when I needed his help in going through the formalities of the admission process. All through this time, my mother supported me with her silent prayers and quiet confidence in my abilities. I remember that auspicious rainy day when I came home after getting admitted to the medical school. She gave me the best compliment, which I shall cherish for all the days of my earth walk. She said: *My son, up to now you have been a piece of raw gold; and now the experiences of life and the medical training will carve you into a beautiful ornament.*

With hindsight, I could say that entering medical school was very crucial to my spiritual awakening. I needed to engage in a profession that I could practise with dignity and honesty and in the process grow spiritually as well. Medicine also offered me the passport to travel to the West, where the rest of my destiny was waiting to unfold, including meeting my spiritual teachers. Even Buddha in his eightfold path emphasized the importance of a proper vocation as a prerequisite to awakening. Had I stayed in my father's business, the nature of the work was such that it would have not only delayed my awakening, it might have even stunted my emotional and spiritual growth.

Medical school was a lively period of intense learning, growing, travelling, playing, and maturing fast from a shy teenager to a young adult fully qualified as a physician by twenty-two years of age. During the final years of medical school, I reverted to the dream of going abroad for further studies, the seeds of which had been innocently planted in my earlier life during visits to the Golden Temple and my mother's dentist. With hindsight, I could also have been subconsciously trying to escape my father's influence, since he kept luring me to come back to his textile business or open my medical clinic as another side business that he could manage. But I yearned to be free from all shackles and follow the guidance of my inner self.

I have since learned that at a soul level there were probably past-life karmic relationships with many souls, including my wife, who were to meet me only in the West. Even though my wife and I were in the same class in medical school, it was only in North America we reconnected in a meaningful way as life partners. Somehow, the Universe listened to my request and created synchronicities of circumstances and a sponsorship. I ended up immigrating to Canada at twenty-three years of age, ready to commence further medical training. As a young adult, I had not given much conscious thought to God. I did not hate God, but neither did I love God. I was just too busy living my life to ponder this question.

When I first arrived in Canada, I ended up of all places in the city of Saskatoon in the province of Saskatchewan. It was my first exposure to the cold, harsh winter in the prairies, where the temperature could go as low as minus sixty degrees Centigrade, especially with the wind chill factor. This was also the city that offered me the indispensable support to get my first residency position in pathology in Kingston, Ontario, through a series of synchronicities. Pathology was not my chosen field, but that was the only opportunity available to me as a foreign graduate to get into the system. Even from a spiritual perspective, pathology was not where my growth lay, but it seems I was meant to meet somebody in Kingston who would introduce me to the grand rounds in psychiatry, and that would ignite a desire within me to make a career of it.

I remember the longest four-day Easter weekend of 1978, when I had the misfortune or good fortune of being on call. I had the busiest weekend ever in the history of the pathology department. I spent almost sixteen hours every day in the basement morgue of the Kingston General Hospital doing autopsies. In four days, I performed or assisted with sixteen autopsies, and each autopsy for me meant spending four hours with a dead body, cooped up in the windowless morgue, with an unhappy, chain-smoking morgue attendant who would rather be at home with his family for Easter dinner. I was expected to figure out all the answers to the mystery of the patient's death (but alas, too late for this knowledge to have any benefit for the patient!). I can still experience the strong, offensive smell of formalin as I recall my Monday evening in the morgue going over all the tissue samples so I could present my findings on the Tuesday morning rounds to all my colleagues and the staff, who would be curious, sharp, and well rested after a four-day long weekend.

I needed to have the contrast of that on-call experience to get in touch with my real yearnings to work with living people, and it inspired me to pursue my growing interest in psychiatry. On Tuesday, immediately after the rounds, I picked up the public phone in the hospital lobby and dialled Dr. Divic's office; he was the director of the psychiatric residency program in Ottawa at that time. The standard response from his secretary was that there were no openings for that year, and to wait until July of the following year. This is where the wisdom (*Dixsha*) that I had learned from my elders came to my rescue. I asked to meet the director anyway. His secretary did not promise me a firm appointment but offered to try if I was willing to show up in Ottawa and take a chance. I had learned to be a possibility thinker by watching my father deal with similar situations. My father was not formally educated but he taught me by example to ask for what I want, not to hesitate or give up easily, and be willing to run the extra mile.

I arrived in Ottawa well prepared for an interview, and that is exactly what happened as soon as I stepped into the director's office. I was still wearing a turban, the traditional Sikh headgear. This led to an unusual connection with Dr. Divic (who passed away several years ago), since the turban reminded him of a Sikh colleague and friend from his training days at McGill University. After the interview, he arranged for me to be interviewed by his colleague Dr. Hymen Caplan (who also has passed away), a world-famous child psychiatrist.

Dr. Caplan started the interview by asking me, "Why do you want to become a psychiatrist?"

In my innocence I answered his question by posing a similar question to him. He spent the next half-hour describing his journey and how he came to choose psychiatry, and that was the end of my interview with him. I did not know what to make of the two interviews, but by the end of the week, I got a letter in the mail stating that quite unexpectedly they had found a position for me at Brockville Psychiatric Hospital for the same year, 1978. I vividly remember jumping with joy at this miracle — until it dawned on me that I had created another challenge to deal with. How could I accept this position when I had another year to go on my contract with the department of pathology?

Some of the staff in the department were not very accepting of the foreign graduates, while others were sympathetic but could not openly support us. Once again, lessons of wisdom learned from the elders (*Dixsha*) came to my aid. I asked to see the chairman of the department, Dr. Kaufman, on a Sunday afternoon at the hospital. It baffles me to till today where I got the courage as a first-year resident to ask my chairman to give up his Sunday afternoon for me. He probably sensed the urgency in my voice and surprisingly agreed to meet me at short notice. I shared my predicament with him as to an elder, a human being, rather than a department chairman. Something in our conversation touched him, and he agreed to set me free from the contract and even blessed me to pursue my passion in my career, which was definitely not pathology. I know in setting me free he probably risked opposition from some members of his faculty who would have stopped me from breaking a contract, had they gotten wind of it. I shall remain eternally grateful to Dr. Kaufman for his kindness and compassion.

Another favourable twist of fate: the psychiatry department found a residency position for me in Ottawa instead of Brockville. The capital city of Ottawa is where I was to spend the major part of the next thirty-two years, learning, growing, raising a family, practising medicine, and awakening. Even before immigrating to Canada, I remember looking at pictures of Ottawa and having visions of already living there. Outwardly it may appear that I have made some choices, yet there are so many synchronicities that I often wonder if the mysterious hand of fate has been guiding my journey all along, and the notion of free will is simply an illusion.

I continued to wear a turban (the traditional headgear for most Sikhs) for the first two years of my residency. The very first day of my residency, when I walked into the grounds of The Royal Ottawa Hospital, a child came running to me, yelling, "Sinbad! Sinbad! Give me gold!" It was obviously the first time he had seen someone in the hospital wearing a turban. He became rather friendly with me and would often come and visit me on the ward. I soon became his favourite "Sinbad doctor."

My patients were often quite curious about me and wanted to know about this man from the East. I was equally curious about them and asked all kinds of simple and sometimes naive questions.

Later on during the residency, I realized that the cultural and background differences actually became a stimulus for more creative and engaging therapeutic encounters. Some of the qualities that clients appreciated were caring, sincerity, warmth, unconditional regard, professionalism, and competence.

I still recall my first long-term psychotherapy client. She followed me through various hospitals during my psychiatric rotation. At the conclusion of her therapy, she told me that it was my sincerity and warmth that kept her involved in the therapeutic process. After the first few sessions, our cultural differences did not matter to her. She gave me the best compliment one day when she described her experience of being in the session with me as akin to "sitting next to a fireplace feeling warm and comfortable."

Within the first year of my residency in 1978, I entered psychoanalysis for personal growth and to develop keen sensitivity and understanding of my clients by walking in their shoes. The chairperson of our department was a world-renowned psychoanalyst, and personal psychoanalysis was encouraged, a tradition that seems to be dying out these days due to the increasing emphasis on pharmacological interventions.

My first analyst was a very motherly, kind, and gentle lady. She actually introduced me to Dr. Herbert Benson's book, *The Relaxation Response*,[1] based on his research on Transcendental Meditation. Traditional analysts are not supposed to directly offer advice or suggest books like that; they are expected to behave like blank screens on which the clients can project their unresolved issues. But I am glad that she did suggest that book, since it started me on a meditation practice and prepared the ground for further awakening. After six months, I had to look for another analyst, since she moved to another town to follow her husband, who had been transferred. I shall be eternally grateful for that liberating six months of psychoanalytic experience. Not only did it give me a growing sense of inner freedom, even outwardly I felt liberated from the custom of having to wear the turban to work. My faith by now had become an internal experience, no longer bound by the outer rituals.

My second analyst was more like a father — quite a contrast from the previous motherly therapist. I worked with him from 1979

---

1   Dr. Herbert Benson, *The Relaxation Response* (New York: William Morrow & Co. Inc., 1975).

until the end of 1983. Near the end of my psychoanalysis, I began to ask questions of a spiritual nature, while my analyst gave me interpretations and responses, which were probably appropriate for the therapeutic context but did not satisfy my yearning to know the deeper Truth. That was when I began to actively search outside the analytic box for this Truth.

My secretary would often read her *Daily Word* in the morning, and it had become my ritual to review my schedule for the day and hang around the reception desk a little longer to read her copy of the *Daily Word*. Finally she ordered me my own copy of the monthly inspirational publication of the Unity Church, which has headquarters in Kansas City. I also discovered that the Unity Church of Ottawa had a "dial-a-thought" service of inspirational messages. For some time, it became my morning routine to have a cup of coffee and call dial-a-thought and contemplate the inspirational message of the day before starting my clinical work. Finally, I decided to visit the Unity Church of Ottawa.

As it turned out, a visiting teacher from Montreal was giving a series of talks on a book titled *Lessons in Truth*,[2] by Dr. Emilie Cady. From her lectures, I had for the first time a clearer understanding of a universal, all-inclusive God as described in the Bible, Acts 17:28: "For in Him we live and move and have our being." Even in Hindu and Sikh scriptures, God is described as omnipresent and one with His creation. I had no preconceived notions about God, and my mind seemed to be rather fertile and receptive. The universal message of the Sikh gurus and their lives that had surrounded me in Amritsar contributed to my unbiased outlook. So it did not matter to me if I went to a church, a Hindu temple, or a Sikh *gurudwara*, as long as I was learning and growing in my relationship with the Source.

My first meditation teacher was *Sant* Darshan Singh, whom I encountered during my visit to India in 1985. I must acknowledge my wife, Rupinder, for introducing me to him. She also introduced me to the *Hour of Power*, an inspirational broadcast from California by the Dr. Robert Schuller ministries, which I still watch whenever I can. She, too, was on a spiritual quest and had many questions regarding God and spirituality and longed for some wise man to answer them. Her wish was granted when her mother took her to

2   Dr. Harriet Emilie Cady, *Lessons in Truth* (Missouri: Unity Books, 1896).

meet Sant Darshan Singh. She was so moved by his presence that all her questions dissolved into tears of gratitude. On an auspicious day, he initiated us into meditation with a large gathering of seekers from all over the world. After the initiation, he invited us to his private quarters to share a simple yet delicious lunch of curry and rice with him. It was an extraordinary and unforgettable experience of communion with a master. Even though my conversations with him were more at an intellectual and scientific level, my very being recognized his divinity and universal heart. He once wrote us a deeply insightful letter in which he shared stages of spiritual evolution. I never met him again, as he left the physical plane soon after, but his profound contribution lingers on as fragrance in our lives.

We moved to Brockville, Ontario, and from 1984 to 1986, I remained busy, trying to juggle family and professional responsibilities. Life and intimate relationships have been great teachers. They brought all of my ego-based patterns to the surface for illumination, and often the process was painful. I continued to meditate, read, and watch inspirational programs and the *Hour of Power* show whenever I could. Finally, I accepted a staff position in Ottawa, and we moved back here in 1986, instead of to California, Texas, or Tennessee, which had been our other choices. Once again, I wonder if it was all due to the unseen hand and the grace of the spiritual teachers who were waiting for us in Ottawa.

In the spring of 1988, I sought refuge in the Kripalu Yoga Ashram in order to deal with a personal crisis. The ashram is actually an old, well-built Jesuit monastery in the beautiful Berkshire mountains, overlooking a pristine lake situated in the town of Lennox, Massachusetts. One morning at six a.m., sitting near the window of the ashram's third-floor sunroom, meditatively staring at the mist rising from the lake and marvelling at the beauty of the rolling hills, I sincerely prayed for a peaceful spiritual life rather than my ego-based, stress-filled existence. It seems that somebody was listening, since my life experienced a profound spiritual revolution after that prayer. Initially, things got more complicated, yet every crisis brought a blessing.

That same year, I discovered the Sivananda Yoga Ashram in Val Morin, Québec, and that became our holiday spiritual home for years to come. The founder of Sivananda ashrams, Swami Vishnudevananda, inspired us to undergo the yoga teachers' training course in the summer of 1989. A month-long spiritual discipline further fuelled our spiritual quest, and now we were consciously in search of an enlightened master. We were both in a hurry to get enlightened. (I later on realized that in spiritual life, *slow and steady is actually the fastest way to evolve.*)

We made friends with a Spanish couple who introduced us to Sunaina, a Zen teacher in Vermont. Sunaina happened to be a disciple of the famous Roshi Kapileau, known for bringing Zen to the West. My wife as usual dove right into it and even attended a seven-day Zen retreat (*Sesshin*) and started working on her first *koan* on nothingness. A *koan* is usually a question or a statement that is often difficult to understand or resolve with our rational intellect, and therefore the seeker when successful ends up transcending the intellect and gains access to the intuitive wisdom within. A common *koan* is, "*What is the sound of one hand clapping?*" I hesitatingly decided to try an all-day sitting, hoping the process would somehow bring me closer to my search for an enlightened master. Our Spanish friends in Montreal offered to put me up for the night prior to the all-day sitting and also offered to drive with me the next morning to Vermont where the Zen teacher Sunaina lived and conducted retreats in her home. The evening before the trip, my host couple decided to take me out for dinner at a vegetarian restaurant operated by disciples of Sri Chinmoy.

The restaurant had photographs of Sri Chinmoy displayed all over the walls, showing him lifting an incredible amount of weight — something like over 7,000 pounds of weight over his head in a military press style. I had two thoughts simultaneously: either the whole thing was rigged, or there was something that I didn't understand. I decided to buy his book on meditation and spent the rest of the evening until late that night deeply immersed in his consciousness. I felt an unusual connection with him, and the message in his writings seemed to resonate with my inner wisdom. Coincidentally, I had been listening to his simple yet soothing spiritual music for a couple of years without ever knowing anything about him or his path.

The next day, I arrived at the all-day sitting in Vermont, hoping for some guidance from the teacher. In between the several silent meditation sittings, I did get the privilege of a private interview with the Zen teacher. I had several questions about

Zen, and somewhere in the conversation, I asked her about Sri Chinmoy. She told me that in her view, Zen is the most direct path to the truth. She seemed to be quite familiar with Sri Chinmoy and his teachings and suggested that I talk to the wife of the Zen master Roshi Kapileau, who coincidentally happened to be living in Ottawa at that time and apparently had been a senior disciple of Sri Chinmoy.

It seems the universe was arranging all these coincidences for us to connect with Sri Chinmoy. I still remember the incredible joy I felt when I first heard the news of our being accepted by him as his disciples. My wife went to New York first to check him out. It seemed that meeting him challenged all her preconceived notions of what a realized master should look like. By now she was not getting anywhere with the Zen and found it somewhat dry and too wilful for her temperament. Sri Chinmoy's path of love, devotion, and surrender was instantly appealing to her Indian soul. Somewhat prepared by my wife's forewarnings, I was not as shocked to see a realized master dressed in a colourful track suit playing tennis and lifting people[3] in the daytime and in the evening meditating soulfully, and offering peace to the public and his disciples through a concert.

For a while, it seemed we had found what we were looking for: a modern-day spiritual master who claimed to be fully realized. His disciples were all extraordinary people. Among them were celebrities, marathon runners, Olympians, musicians, and special ordinary people, but they all had one thing in common: their dedication to the spiritual life. My children still recall our Friday night drives from Ottawa to Queens, New York, visiting Sri Chinmoy at the tennis court on Saturday and Sunday mornings, staying at Adria Motor Inn, indulging in a breakfast of bagels and *prasad* (blessed food), and returning home late Sunday evening, tired yet spiritually uplifted and ready to carry on with life as usual on Monday. I even had the rare privilege of travelling with Sri Chinmoy on a memo-

---

3   Sri Chinmoy would lift people as his way of honouring them for their positive and noteworthy contribution to the cause of world peace. His disciples had constructed a platform with an attached staircase for lifting people. The person or persons to be honoured would climb up the steps and come to stand on the platform, and Sri Chinmoy would stand under it and push the platform up with the attached bar in a standing overhead press. I have personally watched Sri Chinmoy lifting up to four persons at the same time after a peace concert in Berlin.

rable European tour, the year after the Berlin wall came down. He gave concerts in Berlin, Budapest, and Prague, and lifted many people after the concert simply to honour them for their contribution to world peace.

Sri Chinmoy rarely spoke with his disciples in the first few years. Surprisingly, he acknowledged my wife and me after the European trip by asking us to come up to him at the tennis court and blessing us with a meditative gaze into our eyes. Only in books had I heard of the power of a realized master's gaze. Shortly after that incident, my meditations became very soulful, and poetry started to pour out as though some fountain of creative consciousness had been opened up.

Guru's path was very dynamic, and there was always something happening, such as concerts, peace runs, or his setting a new record in his millions of bird drawings. Most of the disciples on his path happened to be single, so they could dedicate their entire lives to their spiritual unfoldment.[4] For us as a couple, it was difficult to balance family life with his path. Also, we were becoming prey to jealousy from other disciples, since he had obviously showered more attention on us than expected. Guru inwardly recognized our struggle and liberated us by sending us a message that it was time for us to move on. It felt like a rejection, but with hindsight it was like mother eagle pushing the little eaglet off the cliff so that it can fly. He continues to be our guru at an inner level since 1989, even though outwardly we have no longer been active disciples since 1993. His physical form passed away in fall of 2007 and yet he is as alive for us as he ever was.

For my multi-dimensional, interfaith evolution, my soul needed to explore other paths such as Siddha Samadhi Yoga, Syda Yoga, the Self-Realization Fellowship, A Course in Miracles, my own Sikh tradition, the Hindu tradition and scriptures such as the *Bhagavad-Gita*, the kabbalah (from the Jewish mystical tradition), Buddhism, and Sufism. Sri Chinmoy had freed me from the need to have an

---

4   For many of the disciples, their whole life revolved around the Path, which usually involved weekend drives to New York, and volunteering in centre activities as well as spending at least a couple of hours of daily spiritual practice in the form of meditation and reading. Some disciples had taken up running or a creative pursuit as a form of spiritual discipline.

outer teacher by forcing me to trust the teacher within me. *That is what a true guru or a therapist must do: encourage self-reliance rather than dependence.*

On my journey, I also learned from many masters and remain eternally grateful to all of them. Some of them are: Swami Sivananda, Swami Vishnudevananda, Satguru Sivaya Subramuniyaswami, Swami Ramdev, Gurumayi Chidvilasananda, Yogi Desai, Gurumata Amma, Rabbi Gelberman, Rabbi David Zeller, Swami Chinmayananda, Paramahansa Yogananda, Br Rolph, Raju Ji, and Yogi Satyam.

Rabbi Gelberman had lost his wife and only daughter in the holocaust, but when I met him at the Sivananda Yoga Ashram in the Bahamas, he was a joyous and inspiring person. He had learned to live in the present and had made peace with the past. It was he who inspired us to attend his all-faith seminary and become interfaith ministers in 2000.

Side by side with my spiritual quest, I explored beyond my psychiatric training into the Satir model, Gestalt, reiki, hypnosis, Tai Chi, Chi Kung, Ayurveda, and many other complementary approaches. I am deeply indebted to Dr. Wayne Dwyer and Dr. Deepak Chopra for putting in modern-day scientific language some of their insights. The psychotherapeutic model that I have found most spiritually rooted is the Satir model, where the *Self* is at the centre.

Of all the self-help books that I have read, I have found the books by Eckhart Tolle and Thich Nhat Hanh particularly helpful in cultivating presence. Eckhart Tolle's book *The Power of Now* was suggested to me by a cancer patient and the book sat on my shelf for a couple of years until I decided to read it during a trip to Hawaii. Since then I have read most of his books and listened to many of his talks. In 2006, I was gifted a copy of the book *The Journey* by Brandon Bays by a client as a goodbye gift at the conclusion of her therapy. In this book, Brandon Bays shares her personal journey of physical and emotional healing and offers guided introspection processes to access the stored cell memories and empty them out. Once again, some mysterious intuition guided me to pursue this and complete the journey practitioner's program. The journey processes are now a part of my repertoire for personal and professional work.

My spiritual journey has been very rich with experiences. Our rabbi friend David Zeller from Israel would refer to these experiences as receiving *Postcards from Heaven.* But it is not necessary for everybody to have experiences. Some people seem to arrive at their liberation without experiences. It is important that we do not compare our spiritual journey with others — something our ego self loves to do. We are God in the embryo form, and Realization slowly grows within us like a flower, petal by petal.

My active spiritual life is now unfolding into a manifestation phase, where I am starting to share my insights with the world through my talks, presentations, CDs, writings, and so forth. For me, the guru is the whole universe, and I am open to learning from whoever is willing to teach me. My clients, the participants of my various workshops, people I have met along the way have all been teachers to me. Life is a classroom, and our physical body is a learning instrument. Every situation is a setup for learning. I am eternally grateful to Providence for masterminding my life journey to bring me to a point where I am more and more aligned with His intention. In clinical work, I don't see a separation or a conflict between my medical background and my spiritual life. I can sit with a quantum physicist and look at God as a unified field; or with somebody from the AA tradition, who would rather refer to God as a higher power; or an atheist, who is only comfortable with words such as being, presence and awareness. For me it is very clear that everybody, directly or indirectly, is seeking God. We are like fish in the ocean; we move and have our being in God.

While on one hand there has been a deep spiritual satisfaction, at the same time I am also in awe, in a state of childlike wonder, not knowing what is next. I have a sense that we are going through a very interesting time of spiritual evolution. I hope that this sharing has offered you some inspiration and will give you an understanding of my background as you read the rest of the book.

◌◌◌

Key Insights

1. Even the universe gives in when you hold back nothing and give your very best to some quest.

2. Slow is fast in spiritual life. We are already spiritual beings having a human experience.

3. Every crisis has a blessing. All life experiences can be an opportunity for learning, growth, and awakening.

4. God Consciousness awakens within us like a flower, petal by petal. Just allow it to happen naturally and gracefully.

5. Do not compare your spiritual journey with that of others.

Questions to Reflect On

1. Take your journal and write your own spiritual journey. Reflect on all the teachers, synchronicities, and the lessons you have learned along the way.

2. Who are some of the people that you are grateful for in your evolution?

3. How do you react to stressful situations? Has this way of reacting changed over time?

Awakening Practice (Mindfulness of Breath)

To be aware of your breathing is a simple act of cultivating mindfulness, which is another name for awareness or presence. In the beginning, you would need to practise this in a place where you would not be distracted by phone or other interruptions for five or ten minutes. As you become more adept at it, you could practise this while walking, driving, listening, and even in the middle of a busy shopping mall.

As you inhale, silently say, "Breathing in, I am aware"; and as you breathe out, silently say, "Breathing out, I am aware." After a few minutes, you could even shorten the phrase and say "Breathing in" on inhalation and "Breathing out" on exhalation. As your breath and mind become quieter, you can say only "in" and "out," instead of the longer phrase. In the final phases of this exercise, just being aware of the sensation of breathing at the tip of your nose or awareness of the movement of your belly may be all that is required. Notice the momentary pause between inspiration and expiration. Most important is that you remain aware and watch for any tendency for it to become mechanical while your mind is thinking about other things. Practise this for ten minutes every day for a month without any attachment to the result and watch the miracle of transformation in your life.

3

AWARENESS

Only the day to which you are awake dawns.
Henry David Thoreau

Once a TV show host asked a spiritual master to say something pro-found for the viewers. Spontaneously, the master raised his finger in his usual teaching style and responded, *"Awareness."* Puzzled with the elderly master's cryptic response, the host asked him to elabo-rate. At that moment, the master closed his eyes as though contem-plating on how best to respond to the request. After a few painfully long moments for the host, who was probably concerned with undue silence on national TV and his dwindling ratings, the master opened his radiantly bright eyes and said confidently, *"Awareness, Awareness, and Awareness."* If the TV show host happened to be in unawareness, imagine the uncomfortable and perplexed expression on his face, with perhaps an inner resolution never again to bring these uncommunicative spiritual masters onto his show. Alter-natively, if he was consciously awakening, he would have felt the master's pulsating presence beyond the words and would have been transported into a Zen-like experience of higher consciousness. A somewhat similar response could be expected from the viewers of the show.

I periodically attend a meeting of a local spiritual emergence group. This is an interdisciplinary group of open-minded, spiri-tual professionals. Among them are physicians, yoga teachers, body workers, energy healers, shamans, etc. We meet every so often to explore issues related to spiritual emergence and how best to deal with them. At one of the meetings, I posed the following questions to the group members:

What is awareness?

Can awareness be cultivated?

By their struggle with the words, I became acutely aware of the inadequacy of language in describing the inexpressible. *Awareness belongs to the domain of silence.* This is probably the reason why some spiritual teachers prefer you meditate with them rather than have a conversation, lest you misinterpret the message.

However, the subject of "awareness" is so profound — and being a prerequisite to ushering in Heaven Consciousness — that I feel the inner urge to attempt to illustrate it. Knowing fully well the limitation of language, I invite you, the reader, to actively participate in this inquiry process as I share my insights on the subject. Furthermore, please don't get stuck with words but rather look in the direction to which they point and trust the knower within.

What Is Awareness?

Awareness is what makes us humans different from the animals. It is another name for "presence." It is the space between stimulus and response, the pause between two thoughts. Animals are exclusively in stimulus-response mode. If you throw a stone at a dog, it will bark. There is no thinking in it; it is an automatic, instinctive response. However, we as human beings have the ability to *choose* from many responses to any given situation. In reaction to an angry comment, we may retaliate in anger, stay quiet, smile, be concerned, or simply walk away.

(Yet time and again, we behave no differently than animals.[5] Our awareness is like a flickering flame; it waxes and wanes. Our awareness is undermined when we are tired or under the influence of chemicals. For that reason, most recreational drugs or even many prescription medications with CNS side effects may interfere in the evolution of consciousness.)

Imagine a room where the only window is covered by a thick blind. Even though the sun may be shining brightly outside, the room will remain dark. The pause between the stimulus and response is like the window through which the light of consciousness shines through, depending upon the degree to which our mental blinds are open. Enlightened spiritual masters have a wide pause, as though there are no blinds on their window. Their body-mind field is illumi-

---

5   I must say that there are times when animals even surpass humans in their expression of love, loyalty, and caring. Talk to a pet owner or anybody who has swum with dolphins and they will confirm it.

nated with the sun of their consciousness. Artists have understood this, and that is probably why pictures of saints and enlightened masters from various traditions usually have a halo around their heads to depict the glowing sun of their flowering consciousness.

There are times — especially after a retreat or some spiritual practice — when I am in a heightened state of awareness. At these times, I feel unusually awake, alert, and alive within and to the world around me. A tree, a mountain, the song of a bird, the blue sky, or any ordinary stimulus is enough to trigger a poem or tears of gratitude in my eyes. Somebody once asked the Buddha how the world was different for him before and after enlightenment. The Buddha replied, *"Before enlightenment, the trees were trees, the mountains were mountains and the rivers were rivers. But after enlightenment, the trees are **Trees**, the mountains are **Mountains**, the rivers are **Rivers**."* The Buddha was describing his heightened and transformed perception of reality, which we may experience occasionally. In a heightened state of presence, you can see a whole universe in a blade of grass. How many times have you been captivated by the beauty of the sunset or sunrise? Then there are times you may not even notice it, because you are not aware.

Why Cultivate Awareness?

People often ask me, "Why can't we carry on the way we are made by our creator? Can't we postpone cultivating awareness until the retirement years when we will have more time? After all, what is the rush?"

Let me share an anecdote to illustrate the urgency of awakening for all of us in the here and now.

In 1998, I was invited to be a keynote speaker at a Mental Health Awareness Exhibition in my hometown of Amritsar in northern India. The auditorium was packed with professionals, dignitaries, medical students, psychology students, and lay people. The subject happened to be "mind, body, and spirit model." I was trying to explain the role of spirit in balancing the chaotic mind/body field. Just at that precise moment, the lights went out. It was a total blackout, and there was a pin-drop silence in the room. I asked the audience if they wanted me to keep talking; the reply was a unanimous "Yes!" I talked for a while and then asked them this question: "What do we need most in this dark room?"

The answer was again unanimous: "Light!"

Exactly at that precise moment, the power came back and the room was once again lit up. People chuckled at the synchronicity and even wondered if I had staged this little drama to bring home the point that our mind/body is a dark and conditioned field of habit, and we urgently need the light of awareness to create a life of freedom.

As a psychiatrist, every day I hear people's distressing life stories: their shattered dreams, countless sufferings due to physical and/or mental illness, unsatisfactory life situations, and endless struggles in their lives. Many of them would refer to their experiences as no less than hell on Earth. If you were to see these people on the street, they may appear outwardly quite normal and successful, but in my office, when the mask comes off, the first noble truth of the Buddha that "Suffering is Universal" becomes self-evident. Henry David Thoreau alluded to the same truth when he said, "The mass of men lead lives of quiet desperation." Yogis have stated boldly, "*Sarvam Dhukam*," meaning everybody suffers. Even the founder of the Sikh religion, Guru Nanak Dev, said *"Nanak dhukia sab sansar,"*[6] meaning, "the whole world suffers."

Just like everyone else, my clients are all yearning for healing, relief, peace, love, joy, purpose, freedom, prosperity, and being fully alive. For them it would be no less than a miracle similar to ushering in Heaven if their yearnings came true. It is painfully obvious to me that Heaven cannot descend in our lives if we remain in the darkness of unawareness. The suffering in the world is a bottomless pit, and we cannot remove the dark night of ignorance by fighting it. Only when the awareness sun dawns does the night begin to disappear. In my office, there is a plaque on the wall hanging along with my professional certificates, a rather bold and courageous step for me. The plaque has a quote by the famous yogi Paramahansa Yogananda: *"Everything else can wait but our search for God cannot."* Since we all

---

6   The word "*sansar*" means "the world." A note on spelling: there are
     various spellings for words that can be Sanskrit or other Indian languages.
     For example, "*sanskar*" (which has a different meaning than *sansar*) is
     the spelling for the Gurumukhi language, but it is spelled "*samskar*" or
     "*samaskar*" in other Indian languages. Please see the Glossary.

desire an end to the suffering night and yearn for Heaven, therefore it becomes extremely urgent that we invite the light of awareness (God) into every aspect of our lives.

All psychotherapy, when effective, must also lead to expansion of awareness as well as a constructive shift in perception and behaviour. *Awareness is not only an illuminator of darkness; it is also a teacher, a healer, and a transformer.* When the awareness grows to its fullness, one comes to recognize the truth in the profound Sanskrit mantra "*Soham*," meaning "I am Divine; I am that which I have sought. I am awareness beyond form."

The first time I heard this mantra was in 1988 during the final relaxation at the end of a yoga class at Sivananda Ashram in Val Morin, Québec. It was a cool spring morning in the Laurentian Mountains. The yoga class was held in the cozy comfort of the room above the kitchen. Our yoga teacher spontaneously started to chant this verse to gracefully wake us up from deep relaxation. His voice was melodious and the words so profound that a wellspring of joy bubbled up within me. Since that incident, this chant by Swami Sivananda has been very close to my heart.

> *So ham, So ham, Soham Shivoham.*
> *So ham, So ham, Soham Shivoham.*
> *I am not this body, this body is not me.*
> *I am not this mind, this mind is not me.*
> *I am not these thoughts, these thoughts are not me.*
> *I am not these emotions, these emotions are not me.*
> *Sat Chit Ananda, Immortal Bliss I am.*
> *Sat Chit Ananda, Immortal Bliss I am.*

I have been blessed with many such transformative experiences and have come to know for myself without a shadow of a doubt that our true nature is peace, love, and joy, just as the nature of sun is heat and light. *Peace, love, and joy are not like other ephemeral emotional experiences.* We experience them when we are in touch with our *Self.* As we connect with our *Self* on a more regular basis, we start to remember our soul's purpose. Many of my clients after a course of successful therapy start to explore questions of spiritual nature such as,

Who am I?

What is my life's purpose?

Is there a God?

Where do I fit in the grand scheme of things?

Before addressing the question of how to cultivate awareness, it would be relevant to look at the common obstacles to the evolution of awareness.

Obstacles to the Evolution of Awareness

Modern times

A Buddhist's curse and blessing is: "*May you be born in interesting times.*" We are living in a fascinating world of televisions, computers, faxes, Internet, e-mail, BlackBerrys, iPhones, iPods, iPads, androids, and ever-changing technology. Our nervous system is bombarded with stimuli, demanding immediate response, thereby further reducing the "pause" mentioned above. Music is possible when there is a silent space between notes. If you take away the silence, then all that is left is noise. Similarly, our lives have become noisy. There seems to be a conspiracy against cultivating awareness, which requires one to slow down and do one thing at a time; instead, we are pushed into multi-tasking. I found it comical when I recently saw a young man standing at a urinal in the men's washroom at Nassau airport with his iPhone in his hand. He was typing a text message while answering a call of nature at the same time. Talk about multi-tasking! Many of my clients often complain about slavery to their BlackBerrys or addiction to Internet and media. I encounter many children in the elevator playing with their Nintendo DS or the latest gadget.

I am often asked, "Is technology bad? Should we go back to the simplified life of the past?" In the final analysis, technology is neither good nor bad. It is like music; its quality depends on the player. You can either create a symphony or noise. This same technology in the hands of an awakening person can help speed up his or her spiritual growth.

My secretary, Claudia, inspired by the spiritual milieu in the office, decided to create, each day, a new screen saver with a spiritual thought. Now the same technology has become a friendly reminder for her to be present and a stimulus for higher consciousness. I often use the vibrating timer on my digital watch to create a pause so as to bring my attention to the here and now. I once saw a Buddhist monk using a similar vibrating device, a Motivaider, for promoting mindfulness. The Internet has been used by Oprah and Eckhart Tolle to teach a course on his book, *The New Earth*. Apparently, eight million or more people signed on to this webcast. The question I have for you is, "Are you using technology or is it using you?"

Force of habit

Our mind-body is a conditioned field of habits. We keep behaving like Pavlovian dogs despite our best intentions to change and be free from self-defeating behaviours. Negative habits are like weeds; they do not take any special planting, whereas good habits take some effort and a period of sustained attention to nurture them. It is like planting flowers, which takes patience and conscious watering.

I recently saw the advertisement of a leading newspaper: "Never stop thinking." I know of a colleague: The first thing he does in the morning is to read the newspaper and do the crossword puzzle, along with drinking two or three cups of coffee to get his brain processor up to speed. Our identity is completely intertwined with our ability to think. We believe in the statement that Descartes made: *"I think therefore I am."* Yet it is absolutely clear to me from my own spiritual journey that I am *not* my mind. I have a mind just like I have a car, and it would be sensible not let it run out of control.

Many of us are so uncomfortable with silence that we don't know what to do with ourselves. It is easy for us to turn on the TV or get onto the Internet rather than simply *be*. That is why most businesses have music playing on the phone for you when they put you on hold. So in order to cope with the discomfort of silence and what it may bring to the surface, we have developed countless ways to distract ourselves with music, food, sex, talking, reading, TV, Internet, incessant activity, etc.

What are we running from?

The heaven that we really want is within us. The awakened way to beat the habit force of negative behaviours is to consciously start cultivating awareness. For those who are comfortable praying, a sincere prayer can be the most transformative force in dealing with negative habits.

Unresolved pain and unintegrated feelings

Most people carry a varying degree of unresolved pain from the past. In addition to the past pain, there is usually some accumulated residual negativity from day-to-day life. For most people, this pain is usually dormant and occasionally gets triggered, while for others, it is active most of the time — so much so that their identity has become entangled with pain. In my clinical work, I have noticed that this unresolved pain often behaves like a parasite and stays alive by keeping the individual in a state of unconsciousness. Pain is like darkness. It cannot face the light of awareness. Often people are scared to be silent, lest it might bring some demons from the unconscious to surface. One indicator to me of my clients' growing awareness is that they start noticing things in my office that have always been there. A particular painting or a piece of furniture seems to come alive for them as though they have noticed it for the very first time.

Many people cope with their stressful feelings by suppressing them or distracting themselves. This leads to an accumulation of negative emotional energy in the body. Whenever they try to be silent or experience a massage or some type of body work, the first thing that surfaces are these repressed emotions. Sometimes people get discouraged and give up on their inner journey, drawing the erroneous conclusion that meditation was the cause of this. It is like blaming the mirror for showing you the blemishes on your face.

A few years ago, I was coaching a group of health professionals on the benefits of meditation. After a few minutes of practice, most people in the group felt relaxed and more peaceful. However, one member of the group complained that meditation actually made her uncomfortable, since she became aware of all the aches and pains in her body that she had not noticed prior to meditation. In reality, the aches and pains had always been there — they had been covered up by a veil of unconsciousness generated by excessive mental activity. If this person were to persist with a regular practice with non-attachment to the result, eventually not only would she experience the gift of silence but also a deep healing of the body and mind.

Drugs, alcohol, and other chemicals

We live in a society where no celebration is possible without the use of some chemical. It would be truly amusing to watch the Grey Cup or a soccer match being celebrated with ginger ale or orange juice instead of the traditional champagne and beer. The use and abuse of psychoactive substances, recreational drugs, and alcohol is rampant. To a certain degree, it is even socially acceptable. There has been a lot of lobbying, both in Canada and the United States, to legalize marijuana. The drawback is that these chemicals may be a hindrance to the evolution of awareness and interfere with the functioning of the prefrontal cortex, which is the CEO (chief executive officer) of our brain. Many prescription drugs, especially CNS (central nervous system) depressants, anticonvulsants, or other drugs with a CNS side effect, may keep the person stuck at a certain level of emotional and spiritual maturity.

It is certain that by aging we will all grow old and develop grey hair and wrinkles, but that is not a guarantee that we will mature emotionally and spiritually. In order to mature, we need to be able to perform self-reflection, which allows us to learn from the past and make appropriate changes in our life. The act of self-reflection is most effective when done in a non-judgmental state of sobriety. I am not suggesting that the reader become fanatic about even taking a prescription drug or an occasional drink or a glass of wine.

Mind: our best friend or worst enemy

The real culprit behind the mask of above-mentioned obstacles to awareness is our conditioned mind or ego. It is that aspect of mind that creates a sense of separation, conflict in relationships at an interpersonal level, and wars at an international level. It is like an octopus with many tentacles. The emotional and behavioural expressions of this egoic mind can be summarized as,

Kam (Desire)

Krodh (Anger)

Lobh (Greed)

Moha (Attachment)

Ahankara (Pride)

Avarna (Ignorance)

As long as egoic consciousness is driving us, we are preoccupied with security, sensation, and power issues. Our sense of time is past or future and rarely the present moment. It is this ego that keeps pain alive and even creates a victim identity. We use the present moment in order to get to some place or other. The ways of the ego are so pervasive and cunning. The awakened aspect of the same mind now can also liberate us from the clutches of the ego. The mind is like a "lock and key": you can lock yourself into suffering or liberate yourself from it, depending upon which way you turn the key.

This reminds me of the movie *Devil's Advocate*, in which the main actor, Keanu Reeves, portrayed a lawyer who was tempted by the devil. After a moment of conscience, he decided to say no to the temptation and took a stand in favour of truth in court. After the court session, the devil (Al Pacino) came to him disguised as a reporter and massaged Keanu Reeves's ego for having conscience as a lawyer and managed to enrol him for an exclusive interview. The movie ends with the reporter smiling devilishly toward the audience and saying, "Vanity is definitely my favourite sin!"

Vanity is the hallmark of the ego. The egoic self is really an illusion and is born out of identification with our thoughts and feelings. The ego is not our friend, although it claims to be. The word EGO can be an acronym for *Everything Good Out* or *Exiting God Out*. In some Eastern scriptures, it is even referred to as the greatest enemy (*Maha shatru*). This issue is so significant that I have dedicated a whole chapter to it, entitled, "Dance of Two Selves." How to cultivate awareness has been explored in the chapter entitled, "How to Awaken."

Key Insights

1. Awareness and our ability to cultivate it is what make us unique among the animal kingdom. Other commonly used terms for it are presence and mindfulness. If you want to have freedom from suffering, or to prevent it in the first place, then cultivate awareness.

2. Our everyday life and the distractions in the modern world lead to the numbing of our consciousness, and that can create obstacles to the evolution of our awareness.

3. In our attempts to cultivate awareness, we are up against our

own mind, which can be our worst enemy or best friend.

4. Peace, love, and joy are the nature of the self.

5. Technology is neither good nor bad. The outcome depends on the consciousness of the person using it.

Questions to Reflect On

1. How would you rate yourself on a 1 to 10 scale of awareness, where 10 is most aware?

2. How is your relationship with technology? Are you using it, or is it using you?

3. How do you feel being alone with yourself?

4. Do you use any chemicals or drugs often? How are they impacting your emotional and spiritual development?

Awakening Practice (So Ham Meditation)

Find a comfortable position and sit with your back straight. Switch off your phone and make sure you won't be distracted. Breathe normally and notice the breath as you are inhaling and exhaling for a few breaths. Now repeat silently the mantra *So* when you breathe in and *Ham* as you breathe out. (The word *Ham* is pronounced more like "hum.") If your mind wanders, gently bring it back to the mantra. Do this for five to fifteen minutes and enjoy the outcome as a blessing without judgment or comparing the results with your other meditations. The repetition of the mantra is not so much a pronunciation of it but more an idea of it. It is gentle and effortless, like mist rising from a lake. The Sanskrit mantra means, "I am Divine."[7]

---

7   See the Glossary for an in-depth understanding of this mantra.

THE DANCE OF TWO SELVES

*Each of us is two selves. And the great burden of life
is always to keep that higher self in command.
Don't let the lower self take over.*
Martin Luther King, Jr.

Over the years, as a seeker of truth and an interfaith minister, I have explored many spiritual paths and most of the major religious traditions, a quest that was inspired by my personal psychoanalysis. Among the various traditions, I have observed a golden thread of wisdom so profound and transformative in its impact on my spiritual evolution that it deserves an in-depth exploration. This profound wisdom is the *notion of two selves*, a real self (I) and an illusory self (i). In everyday language, the real self has been often referred to as the Higher Self or Being and the illusory self is synonymous with the ego or the mind. A helpful way to imagine the two selves is to consider the metaphor of the sun and the moon: They both shine, but the sun (real self) is self-effulgent, while the moon (illusory self) merely reflects the sunlight and waxes and wanes during a lunar cycle.

Interfaith Perspective

The Vedas, ancient Hindu scriptures, describe the same insight of two selves in a parable of two birds in the *Shwetasvatra Upanishad:* *"There are two birds of a similar plumage sitting on a tree; one eats the fruit of pleasure and pain and the other one watches."* The bird that eats the fruit of pleasure and pain is the ego self, whereas the bird that watches is our Higher Self or witness consciousness.

The ancient Indian epic *Mahabharata* has a similar story, told as a conflict between two clans. The *Kaurvas* represent the forces of darkness (ego) and the *Pandvas* embody the forces of light (real self) and are hence favoured by Lord Krishna, the Divine Self. In the battle, the forces of light (*Pandvas*) prevail over the forces of darkness

(*Kaurvas*), and thus righteousness (*Dharma*) is restored to its proper place.

In the Sikh faith, there is a similar understanding of two selves as *Gurumukh*, guided by the wisdom of the Higher Self or the soul, and *Manmukh*, directed by the mind (another name for the ego). Sikhs are encouraged to lead a balanced life guided by their Higher Selves (*Gurumukh*), living in the material world while deeply rooted in their spirituality, like a lotus flower that lives in the muddy water, drawing nourishment from it, yet remaining untouched by it .

Kabbalah, a mystical tradition of Judaism, describes the two selves in the parable of two trees in a garden: the *tree of life* versus the *tree of knowledge.* The tree of life provides life and sustenance, whereas the tree of knowledge can only offer you concepts and ideas. Just imagine walking into a restaurant and the waiter offering you a choice between eating a real meal prepared from live food versus taking home an illustrated, colourful cardboard menu of the same meal!

A Course in Miracles is a channelled scripture transcribed by Helen Schucman and is based on the teachings of Jesus. The course encourages the reader to live a life guided by the "right mind" (*Holy Spirit*) instead of listening to the demands of our "wrong mind" (ego self).

In the book *Conversations with God*, the author, Neale Donald Walsh, describes the two selves as being either motivated by love or fear. Eckhart Tolle, in his popular book, *The Power of Now*, refers to the two selves as mind or ego versus being. This theme of two selves has found an expression as "the forces of darkness versus the forces of light" in popular movies like *Star Wars* and *Lord of the Rings.*

At the end of one of my workshops, a physician approached me to tell me about a book titled, *The Little Me and the Great Me*, by Lou Austin. She claimed to have relied upon this short book to raise her children and was apparently successful in imparting to them the understanding of the two selves. Upon reading this book, I, too, was impressed by the author's talent in elegantly and effectively expressing the same notion of two selves in a beautiful way, with illustrations and content suitable for children and adults alike.

Freudian Perspective

Allow me at this juncture to make a distinction between the Freudian use of the word "ego" and how it is used it in the context of this book. Freud used *ego* as that part of our mind that allows us to balance and cope with the pressures of our basic instinctual drives (*id*) and the demands of the critical part of our mind (*superego*). Freud's model is limited to mind only, and there is no place for Higher Self or Being. Probably that was the reason why Freud's close associate, Carl Jung, broke away from him in order to accommodate his spiritual outlook.

Synonymous Terms

For the purpose of this chapter, I am going to use the word **ego** as synonymous with *mind, intellect, the thinker, the illusory self, lower self, little me, lower power, fear-directed self,* Manmukh, *the tree of knowledge, the bird that eats the fruit of pleasure/pain, and the forces of darkness.*

The word **being** is synonymous with *Soul, heart, love-directed self, the knower, the real self, the Higher Self,* Gurumukh, *the tree of life, the bird that watches, and the forces of light.*

Being and Ego on a Continuum

Being and ego are not necessarily in opposition, although they could be. This duality of two selves is a subjective reality and is more like a continuum or a scale, where ego is at one end and being is at the other end,[8] and we may go up and down this consciousness scale moment by moment. Even enlightened masters have a thin veil of the ego left that allows them to dwell in the mystical realm and still be functional and practical in the world.

A Frequent Question

My clients frequently ask me: "How do I know which self is driving me?"

The answer is actually very simple. Just pay attention to your feelings and body sensations. If you experience anything other than comfort, love, peace, joy, and gratitude, then the ego is in the driving seat. It is the ego that never stops thinking and needs incessant

---

8   In Nichiren Shosshu Buddhism, there are the Ten Worlds: Hell, Hunger, Animality, Anger, Humanity/Tranquillity, Heaven/Rapture, Learning, Realization, Bodhisattva, and Buddhahood. One can move up and down all ten worlds every day.

stimulation of newspaper, media, Internet, telephone, advertisements, crossword puzzles, Sudoku, or whatever it can feed on. The end result is that our minds are excessively active and often out of control, and we don't know how to turn them off, especially when we need to rest or sleep. The thought-cloud generated by this mental activity veils our joy, which we are all consciously or unconsciously seeking. We identify with our mind so much that we are willing to argue with another person for a point of view. We see a different opinion as a personal insult. The ego needs to have the last word. Only when we consciously slow down our mind do we start to notice its habitual and dysfunctional ways. *Just like when we slow down or stop a ceiling fan, it is possible to see the wings, notice the nuts and bolts, and read anything printed on the wings. The degree to which you can observe your mind and its content of thoughts, feelings, and body sensations depends on your degree of presence/awareness.* One of my favourite metaphors is to see *being*, or unconditioned consciousness, as a vast sky; and *ego*, or conditioned consciousness, as a passing weather front.

Let us now explore together in greater depth the dance of these two selves and how they influence different aspects of our lives.

Ego versus Being

The map of life

The map of the ego self is driven by the senses and therefore it is outward-directed and object-oriented; we seek the Kingdom of Heaven outside us in our worldly activities and material pursuits. The ego-directed map of life is that of *Have/Do/Be*. We need to succeed, get an education, accumulate material comforts, earn name and fame, and become somebody important before we see ourselves being able to have a relaxed, fulfilling, and happy life. In the egoic mode, we have to jump through many hoops, overcome hurdles, and fulfill many conditions before we can be finally happy at some distant date in the future. The end result is that we spend a lifetime chasing "happiness" in outer things, accomplishments, name and fame, an ideal relationship, and more and more material stuff. No wonder even in these hard economic times there has been construction of several new storage facilities in the city of Ottawa to deal with the problem created by an excess of material stuff!

Even when we reach our goals, whatever they may be, the pleasurable feelings are usually transitory, followed by emptiness and the need to strive again for something more. Therefore, the perpetual search for this elusive happiness continues. No wonder we get worn out, stressed, imbalanced, unwell, and even clinically sick in chasing happiness outside of ourselves in the world. No one, regardless of his or her extraordinary worldly accomplishments, has been able to find lasting peace and happiness in the ego's paradigm. You just have to read the newspaper and notice the evidence in the lives of celebrities like the late Michael Jackson, Tiger Woods, the late Lady Diana, and many more rich and famous people. The world in the ego's map can offer us only short-lived pleasure followed by inevitable pain. The tragedy of this paradigm is painfully obvious in the following example.

> John is a single young man in his mid-forties. He has been materially successful in worldly terms, but things no longer make him happy. He spent our whole session crying like a child at the vanity of his life. Physically, he is in terrible shape, with a long list of medications. Emotionally, he is perpetually anxious and depressed. He feels alone and lost. His money can buy only expensive cars, jewellery, an oceanfront condo, medications, paid sex, and the lifestyle of a rich and famous person. But what he yearns for is balance, genuine love, happiness, purpose, and fulfillment. How does one tell this person that the map of Have/Do/Be is a lie? He needs to take a U turn and seek the Kingdom of Heaven within. He needs the Self.

The map of life in the *being* consciousness is completely opposite. It is the self-directed map of *Be/Do/Have*, where the Kingdom of Heaven is sought within, just as the scriptures have been teaching us. A person established in this paradigm starts out by being still and connecting with the peace, love, and joy that are always experienced within, since it is our essential nature. From a place of wholeness of being, he may happily pursue a goal or take action and can end up having all the material and worldly needs fulfilled in a natural and effortless way. It is very apparent to the person in the being-consciousness that his true nature is in fact peace, love, and joy; hence the world of form cannot offer him that which is already within him.

A familiar public example of this paradigm is that of the life story of Eckhart Tolle. Prior to his spiritually transformative experience, he was apparently chronically anxious and depressed, trying to pursue an academic career. One of his spiritual experiences was so complete that the hold of his ego dissolved for good, and he was established in a permanent state of peace and joy. He was inwardly guided to give up his academic career and move to the West Coast of Canada from England. He no longer was following the *Have/Do/Be* paradigm.

Often he would spend his days sitting on park benches in a state of sheer joy. People started to ask him spiritual questions, since they sensed his peace and joy. In the process, he discovered his new role of a spiritual teacher, which eventually inspired him to share his insights through books and other media. Oprah picked his book *The New Earth* for her Web cast, and I had the privilege of viewing it along with over eight million people in a virtual classroom on the Internet.

Tolle never sought name, fame, or success, yet it all came to him effortlessly as a by-product of living a life directed by his Higher Self. It is not necessary that we all have to give up our jobs or go through some major transformation in our lives in order to live a spiritual life. It is quite likely that outwardly you may keep living the same life, but inwardly there would be a shift in perception and attitude. You may be like the lotus flower that grows in the muddy water, yet is unsullied by it.

Emotional experience and perception of time

The core emotion in the egoic mode is usually that of fear, which includes all of the other negative emotions. In the egoic mode, there may be temporary experiences of pleasure, followed by pain. Ego survives by keeping us in the past and future, paying only lip service to the present moment. When we focus on the future instead of the present moment, we create needless anxiety and stress. Similarly, by focusing on the past, the mind can stir up memories of pain and suffering and, in the process, strengthen the ego self and the identity of a victim. *It takes a considerable degree of awareness to consciously use our mind to focus on loving thoughts and positive memories. In the egoic mode, we don't use our mind at all but instead are prostituted by our mind and senses.*

I often hear from my teenage clients, in discussing their addiction to media, how they might sometimes spend up to twenty hours playing the newest video game or chatting on the Web and finding themselves unable to function the next day due to lack of sleep and sheer physical and mental exhaustion. Most adults struggle with similar challenges as well in dealing with their mind and senses.

In the egoic mode, our reactions to life situations are limited to a fight or flight response or some other reactive response. Our pursuits are goal-oriented. The happiness that we all yearn for is by and large postponed until a later date in the far future.

For example, if you ask any university student, "Are you happy?" the likely response is, "I will be once I get this degree out of the way." Then ask the university graduate the same question, and the likely response is, "I will be happy once I get a good job." And at another time in his/her life, the response might be, "I will be happy once I find my soulmate." The chase for this elusive mirage of happiness goes on and on, whereas in the being mode, our sense of time is in the here and now and our pursuits are process-oriented.

Being-consciousness by its light of presence dissolves the darkness of pain. Our emotional state is that of love, peace, joy, and gratitude. *As I have mentioned earlier, love, peace, and joy are actually not emotions but the very nature of our being, and we don't need any outer reason to be joyful. It is like the Sun, whose nature is light and warmth.* In Being mode, we are happily pursuing whatever we need to accomplish, and there is a feeling of being on purpose. We respond to life situations with awareness, wisdom, and compassion rather than the knee-jerk responses of the egoic mode.

Awareness and behaviour

As mentioned previously, the awareness in the egoic mode is limited, and therefore we react to life, rather than taking the time to pause and reflect before taking any action. The internal state is that of confusion, conflict, and fragmentation. Our behaviours are addiction prone, and there is a tendency toward compulsiveness. Whatever we accomplish is usually effortful and at a significant cost to our health and relationships. Financial accomplishments are usually associated with suffering, fear, pride, and attachment. Because of the fragmented nature of the ego self, we unconsciously sabotage ourselves and in the process waste tremendous amounts of life force. In the egoic state, you could be easily manipulated and are unable to see through the deception due to lack of awareness. In short, it is a stressful way to live a human life.

In contrast to the so-called insanity of the egoic consciousness, in the Being mode, the mind is clear and calm. Choices are made from a sense of inner knowing. We have the ability to pause and reflect on an appropriate response instead of the quick knee-jerk response. Perhaps it is this very ability that allowed Christ to say, while on the cross, *"Father, forgive them, for they know not what they do."* Life becomes a process of *allowing*, as though flowing downstream instead of upstream with great effort. In my own egoic mode, I was unable to complete even a chapter of this book after attempting for several months to write. Yet, when I aligned with the Source, I managed to dictate the first draft of nine chapters in ten days.

When clients walk into my office, they are usually confused about some issue. It is obvious to me that they are in the egoic mode, where clarity cannot be found, since clarity is in the domain of Being. My task as a psychotherapist is to help them to experience the clarity of Being. I use dialogue or a variation of mindfulness to help them access their Being or Source consciousness. There is blossoming of awareness in the Being mode. It becomes difficult for people to cheat and lie to a person who is highly aware, since you grow to be, as the biblical saying goes, *"innocent like doves and shrewd like serpents."*

Relationships

Ego-based relationships are full of drama, conflict, control issues, suffering, and a conditional expression of love. These relationships are doomed to suffer and may even break down unless one or both partners are able to evolve to a higher level of consciousness where a truly enlightened relationship is possible. In the egoic mode, we are more concerned about getting than contributing. There is a sense of separation — of *me versus you* — that invariably leads to an array of defences and games people play. "Being Right" and "Poor Me"[9] are a few of the games the ego plays. Some of the egoic defences are blaming, distracting, projection, denial, distortion, repression,

9   Eric Berne, *Games People Play: The Basic Handbook of Transactional Analysis* (New York: Ballantine Books, 1964).

unforgiveness, and rationalization. Even though these games and defences are unconscious, it does not release us from the troublesome consequences. The emotional pain we accumulate over decades in our ego-based relationships far supersedes the original issue and often leads to the development of a victim identity. Guess who is ultimately responsible for our predicament . . .?

In the Being mode, there is a deep sense of oneness and the experience of unconditional love; the focus is more on giving and forgiving. It becomes obvious to us that in the Being mode, giving and receiving are the same. Giving happens from a position of fullness and is without attachment and expectations. This kind of giving blesses both the giver and the receiver. From this consciousness, it seems ludicrous to play any of the games because of this deep sense of connectedness. *If our teeth bit our tongue, there would not be any grievance between them, since both are parts of the same body. No one would ever go to a dentist and say please take out my teeth because they bit my tongue.* When two people are able to relate in an enlightened manner, all that is experienced is a deep sense of peace and love that transcends time and space. Now the relationship has become a spiritual practice (*sadhana*) and every upset can be an opportunity for transformation. The residual pain, if and when it surfaces, can be quickly dissolved if both partners are mindful and cultivating awareness.

Self-esteem

Self-esteem in the egoic consciousness is generally linked to some outer accomplishments such as material success, academic achievements, physical appearance, bank balance, name, fame, etc. Since the world of form is constantly changing, and nothing we accomplish is permanent, in the egoic mode it feels as though the castle of our self-esteem is built on shifting sand and is therefore always vulnerable and under threat, no matter how many self-help books are read or positive affirmations are repeated.

On the other hand, self-esteem in the Being mode is not an issue, since the Self is already whole and complete and its true nature is love, peace, and joy. In the Hindu Vedic scriptures, the Self is described as absolute Truth, absolute Knowledge, and absolute Bliss (*Sat Chit Ananda*). Preschool children generally don't seem to have an issue with self-esteem, and we are all attracted by the radiance of Source shining through them. It is only when they are exposed to the school system and social conditioning that they start to develop some concerns and anxieties about themselves. In a way, all spiritual growth involves some form of unlearning and deconditioning so that once again we can access our true innocent self.

Pursuit of religion and spirituality

In the egoic mode, even a religious or spiritual pursuit, instead of being liberating, can easily turn into an obsessive pursuit bordering on fanaticism and misinterpretation of the scriptures, in some instances resulting in spiritual casualties. Ego loves to judge, compare, and compete and, in the process, creates further barriers in human relationships. The *holier-than-thou* attitude and *fundamentalism* are the hallmarks of an ego-based religious life. We experience our journey as that of a human being who is shackled by limitations and struggling to be spiritual. Our attempts at self-discipline are effortful and often rigid, and the process feels like an upstream struggle; it is therefore bound to fail eventually.

In the Being mode, the pursuit of a religious or spiritual life can be a natural, liberating, fulfilling, heart-opening experience. *There is a growing sense of oneness consciousness, and you see the world within yourself.* There is a direct experience of the divine, and that makes it easier to decipher the hidden, metaphysical meanings in the scriptural writings, which were not previously obvious in the unawakened state. You no longer confuse truth with untruth. In the Being mode, you are already a spiritual being who is having a human experience, and therefore there is no striving, since you have already arrived. Self-discipline is gentle, effortless, and flexible and it feels like a downstream experience.

An acid test of an authentic religious or spiritual life is to see if there is in you a growing sense of peace, joy, and lightness of being. Examine the quality of your relationships, especially intimate relationships. Harmony within and without is the hallmark of an authentic religious or spiritual life.

Self-care and health

Health is always an issue in the egoic mode, even though there may not be any apparent illness. There is frequently an experience of dissatisfaction, stress, or some unease either at the mental or physical level. Most serious health concerns often are made worse by the compulsive egoic mode and self-sabotage. Self-care is generally neglected or is often a struggle. I know that ego is in charge when I hear a healthy young man complaining about his body fat not being less than 15 percent.

I frequently observe people who have a compulsive need to take care of other people or rescue them from suffering, even at the expense of their own health, and in the process they usually become resentful and may themselves feel like victims in the end. My task as a therapist is to assist them to see the distinction between caring and caretaking. When somebody is drowning and you throw them a flotation board, that is a very caring and responsible thing to do. But if you jump into the pool without knowing how to swim then that is akin to caretaking, and in the process you both may drown. I have to remind them that even the saintly Mother Teresa took four hours a day for her self-care needs. It was very obvious to Mother Teresa that she could not give to the world unless she replenished herself every day with the love of Christ through self-care.

In the egoic mode, we experience lack and limitation in the flow of energy. The ego is like the moon reflecting the sun's light; it does not have its own radiance and therefore it waxes and wanes. In the egoic mode, we are functioning off-line from the source.

True and lasting health is possible only in the Being mode. Since you are on-line with the source, there is an experience of inexhaustible supply of energy. It is not uncommon to hear stories of saintly people such as "Peace Pilgrim"[10] and other monks, who would walk long distances without feeling tired. In the Being mode, it becomes easier to take care of yourself while serving other people as well. There is a natural balance among various aspects of self-care.

The following chart summarizes the essence of the paradigm of the ego versus the Being.

10   Peace pilgrim was a saintly lady in the last century who walked across America on foot on several occasions and engaged people in a conversation on peace. She had deep faith that the Lord would take care of her and never asked for food or shelter. The Source took care of all of her needs, often in a miraculous way. She had so much stamina for walking that even athletes could not keep up with her. She never wrote a book, but her letters are published by Friends of Peace Pilgrim.

EGO   BEING

THE MAP OF LIFE

EGO	BEING
Have/Do/Be	Be/Do/Have
Happiness postponed	Living happily now
Outward-directed	Self-directed
Goal and success-oriented	Purpose and process-oriented

EMOTIONAL EXPERIENCE

EGO	BEING
Fear and its various expressions	Peace, love, and joy
Accumulation of pain energy in the field	Free flow of love

PERCEPTION OF TIME

EGO	BEING
Past and future	Now is all there is

AWARENESS/BEHAVIOUR

EGO	BEING
Limited Awareness	Expanded awareness
Fight or flight or a reactive response	Relaxed awareness response

RELATIONSHIPS

EGO	BEING
Conflictual and control drama	Peace and harmony
Separation consciousness	Unity consciousness
Conditional love	Unconditional love

SELF-ESTEEM

EGO	BEING
Dependent on outer conditions	Emanates from the Self
Generally shaky and unstable	Stable

RELIGION/SPIRITUALITY

EGO	BEING
Holier-than-thou and Fundamentalism	Authentic spirituality
Self-discipline effortful and rigid	Self-discipline gentle

SELF-CARE AND HEALTH

EGO	BEING
Self-care often neglected	Self-care natural and graceful
Health always an issue	Naturally healthy

I would like to elaborate on this insight of the Dance of Two Selves with a personal anecdote.

It was the ninth of January 2003. I had woken up feeling tired and in a somewhat sombre mood. I was in Cancun with my wife, and we were heading back to Ottawa. That day, the weather outside was perfect, which through contrast made my mood even worse; rather than travel, I really wanted to be on the beach, reading a book, soaking up the sun, sipping a margarita.

Furthermore, I had not slept well that night, even with the aid of a sedative. The preceding week in Cancun had not been as restful as expected, and the weather was cloudy on most days. So I was not pleased with the prospect of spending a whole day waiting at the airport, travelling, changing planes at Atlanta, and eventually getting home very late in the evening, probably feeling more tired after a vacation that was supposed to have been recharging and restful.

When I arrived at the airport, there were long lineups, and the Mexican authorities were asking passengers to open up all their luggage for inspection prior to checking in, a source of additional frustration and inconvenience, something rarely done at other airports. I had a déjà vu of the painfully frustrating experience of long lineups and chaos at the airport when we had arrived two weeks earlier.

While waiting, I remembered what I often teach my clients: "Whenever you are feeling anything but peace, love, and joy, it means that ego is in the driver's seat, and the best remedy is to call the Higher Self or Holy Spirit for help." So I decided to practise what I preach and started to invoke Spirit by humming this song: "*Come, Holy Spirit, I need Thee. Come, sweet Spirit, I pray. Come with your strength and your power. Come in your own gentle way.*" I must thank my very dear friend Barbara Reid for teaching me this song.

Within a few minutes, I noticed a subtle shift in my awareness. I was actually becoming more present, my awareness more relaxed and gentle; I was courteous to people around me and felt a growing sense of connectedness with the world as compared to my earlier state of "Don't bother me!" I continued to hum this song internally while going through the check-in, customs clearance, security, and finally, while waiting for the plane to arrive. I was becoming more and more perceptive, and the dark cloud over my mood was gradually starting to lift.

My wife wanted to browse through some of the shops, and I was holding her travel documents. Finally, the boarding started, and my wife was nowhere to be found. Ordinarily this would have caused me to be at least somewhat upset but I continued to chant, knowing that it didn't really matter, as long as she arrived and we were able to board the plane before the final call.

My wife did indeed arrive. I sat in my seat, closed my eyes, and kept humming the song in a meditative way; I created an intention to keep humming it until the plane was in the air. I just wanted to push the spiritual experiment a little more to see what was really possible.

The plane was about to take off, and the pilot announced a problem with one of the wheels; the plane had to be taxied back for repairs, meaning more delay. I could hear people's annoyance, but I kept on repeating the song of the Holy Spirit like a mantra and stayed true to my intention and did not open my eyes. I would occasionally hear comments and people's reactions to this unexpected delay. Yet I stayed in this meditative mode of repeating the mantra of Holy Spirit. The process was no longer an act of will; it was as effortless as flying in space.

I did not even realize two hours had passed before the plane finally took off. I was awakened from the meditative state by a burst of purple light in my forehead accompanied by a deep sense of unearthly joy and knowing without doubt that all was okay. I also knew that we would not be able to make it to Ottawa that evening. In fact, I even had a vision of the room and the lobby of the hotel in Atlanta where we would be staying. With the joy came acceptance and a sense of deep peace. Even the universe seemed to resonate with my joyful mood. The lunch tasted delicious after the meditation, and the movie, *My Big Fat Greek Wedding*, added to this state of bliss. My joy was unaffected by whether we made it to Ottawa or stayed in Atlanta. I stayed in this state of uninterrupted joy for the next twenty-four hours or so.

The vision proved to be true, and we ended up staying in the hotel that I envisioned. A rabbi friend of mine would call this type of spiritual experience of heavenly consciousness of joy and peace as a "postcard from Heaven," a kind of "mini-satori," in Zen terms, which serves as a preview as to what enlightenment can be like and keeps the seeker motivated to keep up with his or her spiritual practice.

What happened to Eckhart Tolle was so profound and complete that not only did he break free from the egoic mind mode but he has continued to dwell in that state of peace and bliss. I believe this is a possibility for all of us sooner or later: to eventually break free from the egoic mode that has so far pulled the wool over our eyes and, in the process, created this illusory and fragmented world experience. For most of us, this process of awakening can be graceful, gentle, and gradual — like the blossoming of a lotus flower.

Awakening is a gradual evolution of awareness from unconscious incompetence to unconscious competence. In the process, we go through conscious incompetence to conscious competence. The best metaphor I can think of is by an author who describes her life's journey in five chapters:

Chapter 1 (unconscious incompetence)

I walk down the street.
There is a deep hole in the sidewalk.
I fall in.
I am lost . . . I am helpless.
It isn't my fault.
It takes me forever to find a way out.

You don't even know what you are doing wrong.

Chapter 2 (conscious incompetence)

I walk down the street.
There is a deep hole in the sidewalk.
I pretend I don't see it.
I fall in again.
I can't believe I'm in the same place.
But it isn't my fault.
It still takes me a long time to get out.

This can be very frustrating for many people because they still keep repeating the same mistake, even though they are aware of it.

Chapter 3 (conscious competence — early stage)

I walk down the street.
There is a deep hole in the sidewalk.
I see it is there.
I still fall in . . . it's a habit.
My eyes are open.
I know where I am.
It is my fault.
I get out immediately.

At this stage, the awareness has evolved to the extent that the individual is able to interrupt a dysfunctional pattern as long as he/she is in a state of heightened awareness. The new behaviour pattern has not yet been fully internalized.

Chapter 4 (conscious competence — final stage)

I walk down the street.
There is a deep hole in the sidewalk.
I walk around it.

Chapter 5 (unconscious competence)

I walk down another street.

At this stage, awareness has fully blossomed, and the new behaviour pattern has become second nature.

— Adapted from *The Tibetan Book of the Dead*

Sant Darshan Singh, one of my spiritual teachers, described the stages of spiritual evolution in a letter that he once wrote to us prior to his passing away.

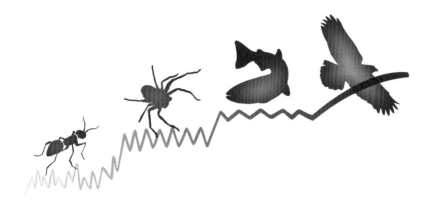

Initially, you are like an *ant* who tries to climb a slippery wall, often unsuccessfully. The seekers in this stage experience frequent ups and downs in their spiritual journey. The next stage is that of a *spider*. Even though the web is flimsy, the spider can move within it more gracefully than the ant on the slippery wall. The seekers start to experience some predictability in their inner life, even though it is still vulnerable to the blows of the ego. The next stage is that of a *fish* that can move up and down the stream with equal ease. The person in this stage of evolution has developed some capacity to deal with the negativity and suffering in the world and therefore may be inspired to get involved in some kind of social reform or movement. The final phase is that of an *eagle*: the infinite consciousness sky is your playground. This is the state of saints and liberated beings.

My intention for elaborating on the dance of two selves is to promote awareness and invite the reader to consciously work toward being guided by the Higher Self and fulfill his or her destiny as an usher of the Heaven consciousness, since lasting peace in the world can come only through us.

Key Insights

1. The concept of two selves is one of the golden threads among various religious and spiritual traditions.

2. If you are feeling anything other than love, peace, joy, and gratitude, that means the ego self is in the driving seat, and it can be a reminder to call for help from the Higher Self.

3. The more you become aware of the ways of the ego, the easier it is to break free from it.

4. Lasting health and well-being is possible only when the Higher Self is established in the driving seat.

5. There is hope for humanity to break free from the dominance of the egoic mode.

Questions to Reflect On

1. "How do I feel right now?" Ask yourself this question often during the day.

2. When was the last time I felt peaceful, joyful, or loving?

3. What am I thankful for at this moment? (Sometimes it helps to put this on paper or in your journal.) Can I be thankful for things that have not worked out?

4. What is the quality of my intimate relationships?

Awakening Practice (Sing and Aspire)

Find a spiritual song, hymn, or chant that inspires you. Try singing or humming it to yourself, especially when you have a free moment or are doing an activity that is routine or automatic, such as walking, driving, washing dishes, or just waiting for your appointments. If you can't find a song or a chant, just repeat God's name or an affirmation or your favourite scriptural quote. You can experience the same aspiration by listening to a soulful recording of a chant by an artist. Eastern mantras such as *Om Namah Shivaya* or *Sat Naam Wahe Guru* are some of my favourite ways to connect with the Divine Consciousness.

HOW TO AWAKEN

*Everything else can wait
but our search for God cannot wait.*
Paramahansa Yogananda

Our body-mind is a dark field of conditioning where most of us struggle with the limitations imposed by negative habit patterns, unable to reach our full potential, resigned to a life of mediocrity and accepting it as "normal" by consensus, since other people are in the same boat. This reminds me of a painting by the famous artist John Pitre portraying a man shackled to the ground by metal chains, struggling to break free, frustrated and exhausted, yet in his vision he sees himself riding the mythical Pegasus, flying above the clouds, free to roam the skies of infinite possibilities. In this dark field of conditioning, Awareness is that light, an expression of Divine Source, a fruit of the spirit that can show us the way, help us break free from the prison of our limitations, fulfill our destiny, realize our true nature, and usher Heaven into our lives and the planet. As suggested in the above quote by Paramahansa Yogananda, our awakening cannot wait.

Sadhana, a Sanskrit word for daily spiritual practice, is the time-tested way to gracefully awaken, sharpen the saw through self-care, uplift our lower nature, cultivate awareness, and transcend the limitations of our habitual nature. Awareness can be cultivated from a flickering flame to a full, blossoming sun with a regular daily *sadhana*.

We are all eventually going to awaken, but it may take a very long time for the evolutionary process. A famous yogi once calculated that at our current rate of evolution, it may take us many incarnations and about 7,000 years of clock time to fully awaken. But with conscious spiritual practice and proper guidance, it is possible for us to awaken in this very lifetime and experience all the joy and possibilities of an awakened life, not to speak of the enormous vibrational contribution to the world.

DIFFERENT STROKES FOR DIFFERENT FOLKS

The ancient seers have noticed differences in people's temperament and have therefore prescribed some variations in the spiritual practice, not unlike a skilled physician who would recommend for two people a different medication for the same illness, depending on the patients' body type, personality, family history, habits, and unique nature.

For those who are heart dominant, the yogis recommend a devotional spiritual practice called *Bhakti Yoga,* involving soulful prayers and spiritual singing, in the process transmuting base emotions to devotion and communing with Source like a lover.

For the intellectual type, there is the path of knowledge also known as *Gyana*[11] *Yoga,* involving contemplative reading of scriptures, meditations, enquiry into the nature of the universe, and using intellect as a ladder, eventually transcending it and opening into Source.

Then there are souls who are restless by nature and are unable to sit still. For those blessed ones, the path of action, also known as *Karma Yoga,* is recommended, whereby the seekers take the spiritual consciousness into their daily activities, and in the process all actions become worship and an offering of service to the Source.

Finally, for those mystical souls with a scientific bent, the royal path of *Raja Yoga* is offered, consisting of an ethical lifestyle, Yoga postures, breathing exercises, proper guidance by a trained *Raja Yogi,* and systematic scientific meditation practice with replicable results culminating in a direct experience of the Divine.

In response to frequent requests, I have described my daily spiritual practice at the end of this chapter, to offer an example of the flexibility that is available in creating a practice that serves you and your unique temperament and allows you to connect with the Divine while living in the material world surrounded by temptations and distractions.

---

11   Also spelled "Jnana."

The prescriptive suggestions in this chapter are aimed at supporting you in your awakening journey, offering you a smorgasbord of options to choose from, creating a practice that suits your temperament and unique station in life, inspiring you to create time for nurturing the soul and stoking the aspiration flame that tends to get covered up with the soot of unawareness caused by the demands of ordinary daily living.

1. Cultivate Mindfulness

Mindfulness is a Buddhist term that has found its way into mainstream psychology and everyday language. There is a growing amount of research done on the physical, emotional, and spiritual benefits of mindfulness, a kind of antidote to the poison of modern living.

Mindfulness is the ability to be fully present in the here and now as you are performing actions without judgment or attachment.

Almost any activity can be turned into a practice to cultivate mindfulness: washing dishes, eating, going up a flight of stairs, listening, music practice, walking, and even driving. Any routine activity can become a mindfulness practice if performed with attention, awareness, and soulfulness, without attachment to the outcome or concern about the next activity.

Let us take washing dishes as an example. *In Zen, there are two ways to wash dishes, the first one being our habitual way, to wash dishes in order to get them clean and to get the unpleasant chore out of the way, so that we can watch our soap opera on TV or whatever other activity really interests us. The second way is to wash dishes in order to wash dishes. The focus is in the here and now, and the act of washing dishes itself has become a practice of being mindful.*

Cultivating awareness of the here and now is a very fulfilling mindfulness practice and is the foundation of all spiritual practices. In order for a car to travel in a particular direction, all the wheels need to be moving in the same direction. Without the basic foundation of mindfulness, all other spiritual practices may feel mechanical and unfulfilling. Past and future are illusions, and Now is all there is. The transformative power of the present moment is further elaborated in the next chapter, "The Eternal Now."

2. Create a Daily Spiritual Practice

The mystical poet Rumi said, *"Find a spiritual practice and submit to it and keep knocking. Someday, somebody will open the door to see who is there."*

The most appropriate word for spiritual practice, already mentioned previously, is the Sanskrit word *sadhana.* This word can be applied to any activity that is process-oriented, e.g., music, spiritual growth, golf, etc. Often, in spiritual circles, people initiate a conversation by asking each other about their *sadhana.* Unlike worldly accomplishments, spiritual practice is not goal-oriented but rather process-oriented, similar to yoga practice, learning to play a piano, or perfecting your golf game. It requires systematic practice, self-discipline, proper attitude of patience, and non-attachment to the fruits of the action.

Spiritual practice may include, among other activities:

Inspirational reading

Prayer

Individual and group meditation

Cultivating mindfulness

Self-reflection

Journalling

Cultivating virtues and eliminating bad habits

Selfless service / charity

Physical and emotional self-care

If you are religious, your *sadhana* may involve reading the scripture, praying in a certain ritualistic way, and attending a religious gathering once or twice a week. Some of the common spiritual practices are described as follows:

Prayer and meditation

Meditation is a ladder from humanity to Divinity; prayers are the arms of the ladder; mindfulness is the foundation on which the ladder rests. When you pray, you speak, and God listens; during meditation, you listen while God whispers.

People often say, "I don't have enough faith and therefore I cannot pray and meditate." Faith can be seen as a muscle that one can build through regular practice of prayer, meditation, and mindfulness. It would seem like a silly excuse if somebody were to say that because she has weak muscles she cannot exercise.

You can find resolution to all your problems by surrendering them to the Divine and consciously connecting with the Source through prayer and meditation.

This is consistent with the teachings of AA's 12-step program. One of my favourite booklets is *The Golden Key*, by Emmet Fox, which suggests a similar solution by asking the reader to "golden key" his problem by thinking about God instead of obsessing about the problem.

I personally favour heartfelt, sincere prayers, in simple everyday language, as compared to mindlessly parroting a ritualistic prayer. If you find it difficult to concentrate, try writing a "Dear God" letter as a form of prayer practice. Many of my clients suffer from concentration difficulties and therefore find it easier to focus through writing a prayer. I have found the *silent unity* prayer service a great resource for creating miracles of healing and transformation. There are studies that confirm unequivocally the positive impact of prayer on a patient's health and recovery. Those patients who had friends, relatives, or even strangers praying for them following a surgery or a major illness often had a better outcome. The silent unity through their dedicated team of ministerial staff offers round-the-clock prayer to anyone who calls them or sends an e-mail. Many of my clients over the years who have tried this approach have predictably experienced a miraculous outcome. Please be aware that I am simply sharing some useful information and not advocating any particular prayer service or spiritual group.

There are so many ways to meditate. Basically all meditations fall in the two broad categories: *concentration and awareness.* In the concentration practice, one needs something to focus on, such as the breath, a mantra, an image, a sound, an object, or a phrase. Concentration practice is like the zoom function of a camera, whereas the practice of awareness is like using the wide-angle view. In awareness practice, there is no specific focus, and all that arises in the body-mind field is observed with compassionate detachment.

In the beginning, it is a good idea to learn a basic meditation technique lasting no longer than twenty to thirty minutes, preferably with guided instructions on a CD. Once you have practised a particular technique for three months regularly, you may be ready to learn another technique. Even after practising meditation for years and having tried many techniques, I find myself coming back to a few basic techniques over and over again.

Cultivating awareness

This is the foundation of all spiritual practice. The words awareness, mindfulness, or presence, are sometimes used synonymously. It is like different flavours of ice cream. The best ways to cultivate this is to give your full attention to whatever you are doing and whosoever you are with.

Inspirational reading

Daily inspirational reading is like planting some flowers in your mental garden. The most effective way to benefit from this practice is to spend some quiet time after the reading so as to reflect on its deeper meaning and explore ways to apply this truth to your daily life. You may use any of the religious scriptures of your tradition for your daily read. I also find it useful to reread my selection a few times during the day. In the Bibliography section, I have included the names of a couple of daily reading books that have been helpful in my journey.

Self-care

Self-care is analogous to tuning a musical instrument. The music of peace, love, and joy cannot play if your body-mind instrument is not properly tuned due to neglecting self-care. Self-care is like sharpening the saw. It is often said that if you have a lot of wood to cut, then you need to spend 80 percent of the time sharpening the saw. Holistic self-care involves physical, emotional, intellectual, social, spiritual, and nutritional care, along with managing your material life, including finances.

People often feel guilty about taking time for self-care. They judge it as selfish, vain, and a form of self-indulgence. I often tell my clients that even the most selfless person, Mother Teresa, would take four hours a day for self-care.

The basic attitude toward self-care is that it is the most responsible thing to do. Self-care comes naturally when we accept and love ourselves and see the Divine in everything, including ourselves.

With that attitude, the human body becomes a temple, a pilgrimage, and a doorway into the universe. A simple test of self-acceptance is to see how you feel when you look at your reflection in the mirror and say, "I love myself." If you can believe it, then it is a positive sign; if not, it simply means that you need to be kind and more loving toward yourself. Self-care requires periodic review, preferably on a weekly basis.

Self-reflection

When we grow old in years, it is definite that we will develop wrinkles and grey hair, but it is not assured that we will mature emotionally and spiritually. It is only through non-judgmental self-reflection that we learn. The Sanskrit word for self-reflection is *swadhaya*. As we reflect on our day and learn from life experiences, there is gradual transformation of our neuronal structure and the prefrontal cortex, which is also considered as the CEO (chief executive officer) of our brain. As our CEO evolves, it impacts our values, mood, concentration, intelligence, creativity, learning ability, relationships, and intuition.

Let us take two healthy persons at age forty-seven. While one of them may be struggling with basic day-to-day issues of survival, the other might be capable of being the prime minister of Canada and ready and able to shoulder the responsibilities of a great nation. One can say with certainty that the prefrontal cortex is much more evolved and integrated in the latter case.

Journalling

The invention of paper has been a blessing and a curse. While we have shelves stacked with books, yet we do not have the presence or wisdom to truly transform our lives as did the wise elders from many traditions who were truly liberated, their minds not burdened by the information in books.

Journalling is one very constructive use of paper. It is a great tool for self-reflection, writing prayers, creating a spiritual diary, counting one's blessings through gratitude, self-monitoring one's practice, and clarifying thoughts and feelings. *In order for the journal to be effective, it is important that it be private.* I have found it helpful to use a hardcover spiral journal that opens flat, is not too big, and is easy to carry around. You can also maintain a journal on your computer and use password protection to keep it private, if that serves you better. (See Appendix B on Transformative Journal-ling and maintaining a spiritual diary.)

Selfless service (seva)

Selfless service is a complete spiritual practice in its own right. Any action taken mindfully without any expectation of reward and as an offering to the Source becomes a selfless action, a form of *puja* (worship). The Sanskrit word for the path that leads to liberation through practice of selfless action is *karma yoga*. It is suitable for all kinds of seekers, especially the action-oriented people who find it hard to sit still. Service prepares the heart and mind and makes it possible for the seeds of awakening to sprout. Service is also the rent we all need to pay for the privilege of living on the planet we call home. The attitude of service is more important than any out-ward action. Even listening with empathy is an act of service. A per-son established in karma yoga sees all actions as an act of worship. He sees the Divine in all creation and for him all actions are an offering to the Lord. The outcome is seen as a blessing of Divine grace — *prasad.*

Loving-kindness practice (Metta meditation)

I have found loving-kindness meditation to have the same effect as selfless service. It softens the heart as you cultivate friendliness toward all creation. Buddha taught this beautiful meditation some 2,500 years ago. The Pali word for it is *metta*, meaning "friendli-ness." The process of meditation involves sending blessings to all beings, including yourself. This meditation is described at the end of chapter eight.

Inspired singing

Soulful singing or chanting, too, can be a complete spiritual disci-pline in its own right. The Sanskrit term for this is *laya yoga.* I am eternally grateful to all of the teachers who introduced me to chant-ing and singing, especially Sri Chinmoy and Gurumayi. Whenever there is a dry period in my spiritual life, reading my gratitude jour-nal, soulful singing, or listening to chanting can quickly and pre-dictably get me back on-line with the Source.

Yoga postures (asanas)

The branch of yoga that deals with physical postures called *asanas* is often referred to as *hatha yoga.* There seems to have been a yoga revolution in North America and the rest of the world over the past twenty-five years. Almost all fitness clubs, spas, hotels, and community centres have yoga classes in great demand. Yogic postures and yogic breathing exercises can assist in the awakening process by preparing the body, promoting balance, cultivating awareness, and opening up the spiritual channels to the flow of subtle energy. It is not uncommon that a person may start yoga practice in order to look good or have a slender body and over time get interested in meditation and the yogic philosophy.

There are so many different schools and types of yoga that it is very confusing for people to choose. The best way to find a class and a teacher that suits you is through trying a few classes by different teachers. A good class should start and end with a prayer and relaxation; and mindfulness practised throughout the class. In yoga, there is no competition or comparison; non-attachment to the fruit of the actions is the proper attitude. Unfortunately, many teaching schools have turned yoga into a competitive, ego-driven pursuit.

Pranayama

Pranayama means "management of life force." It is one of the eight limbs of Raja yoga; a path suitable for people with mystical and scientific tendencies. Pranayama includes a series of breathing exercises aimed at recharging the body and creating a reservoir of surplus energy that can initially help the body and mind to heal and eventually fuels the aspiration flame of the seeker, taking him or her all the way to enlightenment. Pranayama is a very powerful practice and it is essential to get proper instruction from a qualified teacher. Further, it is prudent to combine yoga and pranayama with some devotional practice and spiritual guidance so that the egoic pride, a common side-effect of excessive yoga practice, can be kept in check.

Remembering God's name

The Sanskrit word for this form of practice is *japa.* This may seem like a very simple, straightforward, and effortless practice; nevertheless, it can be very transformative in its impact on the seeker's evolution. I have been very impressed by the story of Br. Lawrence, a

Carmelite monk of the seventeenth century. He did not often attend mass or read scriptures, but resigned himself to a simple practice of remembering God as often as he could; yet he was often in rapture, and even the abbot loved to be around him to experience his divine fervour. The abbot encouraged him to put in writing his practice for the benefit of other seekers. Fortunately, the little book *The Practice of the Presence of God*, by Br. Lawrence, is still available.

Tai Chi, Chi Kung, and martial arts

Tai Chi and Chi Kung are also playing a significant role in the spiritual evolution of humanity by offering very gentle, slow, circular movements that have a profound impact on the living matrix of the human body and its energetic system. Similarly, martial arts, if practised mindfully, can act as a catalyst to spiritual growth by promoting mind-body coordination, self-discipline, and concentration, qualities that are necessary for spiritual evolution.

3. Proper Attitude toward Spiritual Practice (*Sadhana*)

It is very important to remember that spiritual life is a process-oriented journey. Having been good at a goal-oriented approach, I found myself making a five-year goal of enlightenment, only to realize that ego loves to make a project out of enlightenment and, in the process, creates time in order to ensure its own survival.

Seeking enlightenment keeps us in the future and we miss out on the precious now. All that we seek is in the now.

In the West, people have the attitude that if a little practice is good, then more would be better — without realizing that excessive and inappropriate spiritual practice can often lead to spiritual casualties. There is a clinical term for this condition called *spiritual emergence syndrome*, where a person experiences symptoms due to spiritual unfoldment that could often be confused with psychiatric or medical conditions. Under ideal circumstances, spiritual emergence is a sign of awakening, something to be thankful for. But the same awakening can be very disruptive to the individual personally and professionally if the basic infrastructure of the body-mind is not ready. *Slow and steady is the fastest road to progress in the spiritual journey.*

Depending upon many factors, your spiritual journey may or

may not be accompanied by experiences. If experiences come along the way, acknowledge them as "postcards from Heaven" to inspire you. Do not be attached to your experiences, lest they lead you into a detour, thereby delaying your full blossoming — which is exactly what your ego self would want you to do in order to ensure its survival.

People starting a spiritual practice may follow one of the following learning curves, depending on the evolution of their consciousness.[12]

DABBLERS. Those on this curve may be very interested and enthusiastic for the first couple of months, only to lose interest when the next fad comes along.

COMPULSIVE DOERS. Here there is a lot of pull and push. Often people make unrealistic goals that they cannot keep up with and invariably end up giving up on their practice after a physical or an emotional crisis.

HACKERS. These types may continue with their practice, often mindlessly, without making any significant progress. As the expression goes, they just "hack around" with their practice.

MASTERS. The people on this curve show a high degree of presence. They are able to tolerate slow progress and many plateaus along the way. After a couple of years, when everybody else is out of the race, the masters are still making progress. As the awareness evolves, it becomes easier to follow the mastery path.

I had the privilege of interviewing a spiritual woman in her thirties who started running one block a day and gradually over time she increased her distance until, three years later, she was able to run a marathon. In the fourth year, she had an accident and could not walk and had to retrain herself. Within

12 Adapted from the article "Mastery: The Secret of Ultimate Fitness," by George Leonard, published in *Esquire* in May 1987.

another couple of years, she was running marathons and ultra-marathons. By the time I interviewed her in the twelfth year, she had just managed to complete a 1,300-mile ultra-marathon in nineteen days and twenty hours. There was no roughness in her body and there was gentleness in her manners; her running was an expression of her spiritual practice. While running, she would be practising mindfulness and reciting spiritual poems inwardly. She had all the qualities of somebody on a mastery path.

In the spiritual life, there is no competition with anyone; all that is required is to keep on improving one's personal best. Like a man or woman of action (*karma yogi or yogini*), the focus needs to be on the process; all progress is seen as an act of divine grace.

4. Creating a Sacred Space

Having grown up with the tradition of a prayer room in the house, I have maintained this practice in our family life, and we all find it a great blessing. If you don't have a spare room, you can allocate a corner of a room or a closet to set up an altar. You can put those icons, pictures, or inspirational sayings on the altar that motivate you to pursue your spiritual practice with joy and aspiration. Apparently having a sacred place and a set routine makes it easy to overcome the obstacles that sooner or later everybody encounters on their spiritual path. Unless you are a realized master who can meditate anywhere, a clean, uncluttered surrounding with good *feng shui* inspires most people to go within. As one advances in the spiritual journey, a time may come when the sacredness is internalized and you take this quality of *holiness* with you wherever you go.

5. A Day of Mindfulness

A daily shower may keep your bathtub relatively clean, but after a few days, there can be a scum on the surface requiring a thorough scrub. Similarly, daily spiritual practice might keep your system open, but after a few days, we, too, need a thorough spiritual scrub to wipe away the scum of negativity and the residue of mundane daily living that has a numbing effect on our connection with the Source.

This very need is recognized by different wisdom traditions, and they have prescribed guidelines for people to follow, such as the Sabbath in the Jewish tradition. A day of mindfulness — or, as some people would like to call it, a self-care day or mental health day — is a similar idea. To start with, one can commit a half day per week, and eventually work up to one day a week. On that day, the focus is on *being* rather than *doing*. The day of mindfulness can be spent in self-care, prayer, meditation, self-reflection, communing with nature, listening to or playing music, inspirational reading, attending a spiritual group gathering, juice fasting, getting a massage, or visiting a like-minded friend and meditating together. All activities are done in a mindful way and if possible at half speed. A mindfulness day is very deeply nurturing to our whole being and also accelerates the awakening process. Every few months, a retreat for a few days to a week is another expression of the same idea to keep your system open, tuned, and sharpened through self-care. You may not know when God will choose for you to be enlightened. I like the Zen saying, "Be ready for death or enlightenment, whichever comes first."

6. Discover Your Life Purpose

Life is like a jungle, and we need a compass to find our way. Life purpose is the compass that points to our true north and allows us to align all our choices and actions with our highest yearnings. Imagine trying to put together even a basic 500-piece jigsaw puzzle without the final picture in front of you; it would be virtually impossible. *Our life is infinitely more complicated than a jigsaw puzzle, and we need to have a final picture of our life purpose always in front of us.*

Discovering your life purpose involves self-reflection and going within. At a universal yearning level, we all want to be happy, healthy, prosperous, peaceful, loving, and loved; we want to learn, make a contribution, and leave the world a better place. Within this broader framework of being happy and ushering in Heaven on earth, each person has a unique role to play. There are many self-help books on this subject that you can read; or you can attend workshops or find a life coach who can help you to clarify your mission.

Clarifying my life purpose has definitely inspired me to write this book. Once your mission is clear, then it becomes easier to align your goals and other aspects of life with it. A mission/purpose is not a static thing, like a trophy that you can display on your shelf, but rather a living process, like a new sunrise each morning. Therefore, periodic review is essential.

7. Group Practice (*Satsang*)

In order to fly, a bird needs two wings. Likewise, in order to progress on the spiritual path, we need the two wings of individual practice and group support. *Satsang* means "the company of truth." *Sangha* is the Buddhist term for a community of seekers of truth. Weekly group support is recommended; this may be in the form of attending a formal religious meeting or a meditation group. For people who are housebound due to illness, a televised church service or an Internet podcast may provide an experience of being connected with other seekers. Without the group support, most people find it hard to keep up their practice and they start to lose their motivation. We can all learn from our Canada geese, which fly in a V formation. These birds have learned that by flying together, it is 70 percent easier aerodynamically. A spiritual community is like a boat that can help us cross the sea of *samsara* without drowning in the suffering.

8. The Role of a Guru

The word *guru* means "one who removes darkness." Having learned from many masters, I have come to this realization: there is only one guru — our *inner guru* that dwells within us and is often referred to as the *inner pilot* or the voice within.

The role of the outer guru is to assist you to get in touch with the inner guru rather than promoting dependence on him or her.

I have observed that most gurus fall from grace and quite often have some scandals around them. The disciples shower their gurus with adoration and project on them qualities that the guru may not have. It is difficult for the gurus to deal with all the adoration and temptation. Furthermore, they get stuck with the role of a guru and cannot claim to be human. Often many disciples are looking for a perfect parent in their guru.

The guru tradition flourished in India at a time when children would enter the *gurukula* (school) at a young age and would often stay with the guru, who would raise them as a family member. Times are different now. I would like to propose a paradigm of the *guru principle* instead. In the guru principle paradigm, the universe is your teacher as long as you are sincere and receptive. There is nothing wrong in seeking a teacher or a guru at any phase of your journey.

The best advice a wise master once gave about this was, *"When looking for a guru, keep both eyes open. Once you have found your guru, keep at least one eye open."* Simply stated, it means, don't give up your discernment and common sense. In my Journey, having encountered many masters, when faced with their scandals, I was not disappointed. I simply saw them in a more realistic light, in part due to my profession, which offered me compassion, understanding, and meaningful insights into the inner lives of some of the gurus and their disciples.

9. Obstacles in Spiritual Practice

In the spiritual life, you are up against your own mind, which is another name for the ego. The ego is very afraid of the light of awareness, and therefore enlightenment can be perceived by ego as comparable to annihilation. So it creates obstacles in the form of negative feelings toward practice, tiredness, boredom, restlessness, and distractions. *Ego wants to make sure that you remain a seeker rather than a finder.*

Frequently I have noticed that the meditation tape I custom-make for my clients ends up being lost or misplaced, and therefore they are not able to do the practice; once again, ego prevailed, albeit temporarily. A psychoanalyst would call it a form of resistance. In spiritual terms, it is the ego ensuring its survival. If you really pay attention to the struggles in your personal journey, you will notice the dance of two selves at every step of the way. We have within us both the forces of light and darkness. Gandhi said it so eloquently: *"Most battles are fought within our heart."*

It is only through prayer, meditation, cultivating presence, and Divine Grace that this internal battle can be won. A client of mine told me about his Alcoholics Anonymous 12-Step Program. In that tradition, the answer to all problems is to "dial 311." Step 3 of the twelve steps is to "Let go and let God." Step 11 is to "Deepen the connection with the source through prayer and meditation." What simple yet profound wisdom in these steps.

MY SPIRITUAL PRACTICE

My spiritual practice is ever-evolving and over time has become more and more attuned to my unique personal needs as a family man as well as to my professional requirements. I invariably start my day with some uplifting reading, exercise, and twenty to thirty minutes of prayer and meditation. The physical exercise in the morning is usually stationary biking while watching an inspirational video. Depending upon weather or my needs, I may instead go for a walk, practise Tai Chi, yoga asanas, and yogic breathing exercises. Since my work is of a psycho-spiritual nature, it allows me to remain steeped in mindfulness throughout the day.

Once a week, I try to attend some kind of a group spiritual practice, either at a church, a temple, or a *Gurudwara*, depending on what is happening in the community and my needs at that time. If I am not able to attend a spiritual gathering, I might watch a television show of a spiritual/religious nature. Sometimes I listen to my own meditation tapes or recordings of my wife's meditations. Some days I may create variety in my meditations, using music and visual imagery of light. Loving-kindness meditation is one of my favourite practices, especially at the end of the day. With divine grace, I get to pray and meditate usually two to three times a day for twenty to thirty minutes at each sitting. On the weekends, I might sit for a longer period in meditation and often practise yoga as well.

As I have evolved spiritually, I have come to appreciate the value of integrating emotional and energetic experiences through "grounding practice." In this practice, the focus is on the body, so that the flow of light that is being processed through the body is unobstructed. A helpful imagery of grounding meditation is that of standing under a waterfall; or growing roots in your feet and becoming a conduit for energy to flow through you into the ground.

Whenever there is a saintly person or a spiritual speaker in town, I seek his or her company and learn from him/her. Being with saintly people is like bringing a log that is smouldering next to a log that is already burning brightly and, after some time together, they both are burning equally brightly. There is certainly a transmission of consciousness that occurs when you are in the presence of somebody who is highly aware and conscious. It is as though he/she radiates a field of consciousness around him/her where no negativity can survive. The presence alone of the master lessens the power of egoic forces. This may also be the role of enlightened therapists in the coming age. I often teach meditations to my clients and support them in their spiritual quest.

I try to maintain a journal so that I can reflect, review, and learn from life. I also use the journal as a means to clarify my internal state at any time, acknowledge the various miracles happening in my life, note down insights, puzzles, and inspirations, monitor my spiritual practice, and count my blessings.

Swami Sivananda prescribed a path of realization through these simple steps: Serve . . . Love . . . Give . . . Purify . . . Meditate . . . and Realize. I try to approach my work as an act of service. In the beginning, I used to have difficulties finding appropriate times and conditions for practice. But now the universe seems to supporting me by providing me opportunities to stay connected with the Source. The following incident illustrates the value of prayer.

> A few years ago, on my way to India, I found myself praying for some support with my spiritual practice. I had noticed that my spiritual practice would suffer during my trips to India due to a busy social calendar. At the end of the trip, I would often feel remorse and a sense of having lost something precious in the process of fulfilling my social and family obligations. After that sincere prayer, I noticed that wherever I went, people wanted to talk to me about spiritual things. A stranger or relative would come and make an unexpected request for me to teach them meditation or discuss a spiritual subject. My visit to my family now turned into a pilgrimage. Since then I have been going to India every year and it is now a pilgrimage to go back home, visit my relatives and friends, share my spiritual journey, and learn from them as well.

Whenever I can, I make a point of taking a retreat for a weekend or a longer time, usually to an ashram or other spiritual place. We have turned our cottage into a spiritual retreat as well for contemplation and doing our practice. In our home, we have a prayer room as a part of our cultural heritage. I am very grateful that my wife and children have also grown with me spiritually; they are a great support in my journey and keep me on track. I continue to learn and share my journey and hope that this sharing will inspire you to create a practice that you can call your own.

༄

Key Insights

1. Everything else can wait, but our spiritual awakening cannot wait.

2. Whether you want enlightenment, worldly success, or relaxed enjoyment of life, awakening can offer you that.

3. Depending upon each person's temperament, their spiritual practices need to be different.

4. Spiritual awakening is a process-oriented journey. Slow and steady is the fastest road to evolve for most people.

5. In the Guru tradition, the focus is on a person as your teacher, whereas in the Guru principle, the whole universe is available to you as a teacher.

Questions to Reflect On

1. Do you have a spiritual practice that inspires you? If so, describe it.

2. If you do not have a practice, then create a vision of an ideal practice that would empower you.

3. What obstacles or challenges do you encounter regularly in your attempts to live a spiritual life? How can you overcome them?

Awakening Practice (Healing Stream Imagery)

Sit on a chair with your back straight, yet comfortable. Make sure you won't be distracted for the next ten minutes or so. Play your favourite classical music and close your eyes. Let the music wash all over you like a healing stream of sound and light vibration. Imagine a vision of a sunrise or a sunset or a place in nature that you may have experienced; or a pure fantasy. Make this a sensory-rich experience. Feel the aliveness in your body. Enjoy this for five to ten minutes.

THE ETERNAL NOW

Look to this day:
For it is life, the very life of life.
In its brief course
Lie all the verities and realities of your existence.
The bliss of growth,
The glory of action,
The splendour of achievement
Are but experiences of time.

For yesterday is but a dream
And tomorrow is only a vision;
And today well-lived, makes
Yesterday a dream of happiness
And every tomorrow a vision of hope.
Look well therefore to this day;
Such is the salutation to the ever-new dawn!

Kalidasa (translated from the Sanskrit)

As the great Indian poet Kalidasa expressed it so beautifully, today is all we have. We have all heard the Latin expression, "*Carpe Diem,*" meaning "Seize the day." A day might be difficult to seize in the beginning, yet almost all of us, with some practice and coaching, can seize the *moments* in the day. So my motto is, "*Carpe Punctum,*" "Seize the moment." This is another way of saying, *Be Here Now.*

"Now" is the gateway to heaven. Ego or the little me cannot exist for long in the Now. The present moment is the window through which the light of Being can shine. An experience of eternal now is akin to a mini-awakening or, using a Zen term, a *satori*. Buddha in his teachings assured enlightenment (*nirvana*) to his disciples if they could just be in the Now long enough to break free. All healing, transformation, and enlightenment is possible in the Now. God is in the Now. Love, peace, and joy are in the Now. The source of life and power is in the Now. Now is so precious; perhaps that is why we call it the "precious present."

Sir William Osler, the father of modern medicine, shared the secret of his success in this story.

> As a young medical student, I was anxious about my future. I would worry about my professional and personal life. I would wonder if patients would come to seek my services. I was also worried about marriage, children, and the responsibilities of a family man. Then one day I went to the library and read a line by Thomas Carlyle that changed my whole life; it became my guiding slogan:
>
> *Our main business is not to see what lies dimly at a distance, but to do what lies clearly at hand.*

Osler interpreted this as living in the *here and now* in a water-tight compartment by sealing off the past and the future. During his illustrious career, he had a whole encyclopaedia of medical publications to his credit, treated many patients, and founded the Johns Hopkins Medical School. Reporters would often ask him how he found time for all his patients. He would say, "I only saw one patient at a time." He had indeed mastered the art of living in the Now.

What Is "Now"?

Now is the gap between two thoughts. It is the pause of awareness between stimulus and response. As mentioned previously, animals are in the stimulus-response mode. If you throw a stone at a dog, it will bark. There is no thinking or awareness involved, which makes us as humans different. Even as humans, our awareness is like a flickering flame. When tired or under stress, we, too, may behave like a conditioned Pavlovian dog. However, we have the potential of expanding our awareness. Our little flickering flame of awareness can evolve into a sun of consciousness. In one of the Star Trek movies, *The Insurrection*, the eternal now is displayed in stunning graphics.

It is as though there is eternity in this moment; the mind becomes quiet, and there is aliveness all around.

Three Personal Illustrations

The idea of Now is simple, yet subtle at the same time. I have chosen to share three anecdotes from my earlier life to help the reader grasp it.

First anecdote

About twenty years ago, I was travelling in northern India. I had taken a bus from the city of Chandigarh to go to Simla, a resort-like hill station in the foothills of the Himalayas. The bus started at five p.m. and was supposed to arrive in Simla four hours later, at nine p.m. About halfway there, the bus broke down. We were all asked to get off the bus and wait for another bus to take us to our destination.

Unfortunately, the buses that followed were all packed. It was almost dusk. A young man in our group turned on his pocket radio and started listening to commentary of a live cricket match happening in another part of the world. The Indian team was batting. Cricket and field hockey are national games, and usually everything comes to a standstill whenever there is an exciting moment in the game. We all forgot our predicament and instead were glued to the radio, totally unaware of our surroundings.

At nine p.m., the last bus came and it, too, was full. The conductor had mercy on us and, against safety regulations, asked us to hop on. We were packed like sardines. There was no room for anybody to move. The conductor sat in the middle of the bus and started to sing popular movie songs that everybody could join in on. Somebody played the beat on the back of a clipboard. For two hours, as the bus was climbing up the hill, there was a magical singalong with lots of laughter. I can still vividly recall the feel of the cool mountain breeze, the melodious voice of the conductor, the smell of pine trees, and the ethereal brightness of the full moon. I arrived at my destination quite late — joyous and fulfilled. We had all experienced the eternal Now. A potentially frustrating situation had turned into a memorable adventure.

Second anecdote

This happened some twelve years ago during another trip to India on my way to visit family. I was at the New Delhi railway station waiting for the train to Amritsar. There was still an hour to wait. The station was bustling with people with no place to sit. I had not slept the previous two nights, due to the seventeen-hour flight from Canada. My body and mind were experiencing jet lag, and I was not very happy at the prospect of waiting for another hour.

Within the preceding twenty-four hours, I had changed countries, time zone, weather, culture, and language. So my system was in shock. Simply speaking, I was not a happy camper and felt disconnected from everybody around me. I needed to be watchful of my luggage. All I wished for was a place to sit and sleep. I wondered how anyone could be peaceful and stay present in this situation.

I found myself praying for grace to show me a way to be peaceful and accept the situation. A silent voice whispered, "Sing the Lord's name." Soon I started to hum some of the one-line songs from various spiritual traditions. I kept humming and pacing up and down the platform while keeping a watch on my luggage. Within a few minutes, the aspiration flame had returned. I started to see the people around me with loving eyes.

There was a young, innocent, baby boy playing on the floor, unaffected by the surroundings. His whole world was there — his parents were also sitting on the floor, keeping watch on him. He had soiled himself, so the mother decided to wash him with water from a container, right in front of everybody. I felt no judgment, as though I were watching the childhood play of Lord Krishna or baby Jesus himself. My eyes welled up with tears of gratitude.

Time passed by quickly, and I forgot all about my jet lag and miserable state. There was a sense of peace and acceptance of the present moment. The train finally arrived, and I peacefully boarded the air-conditioned coach. This shift in consciousness stayed with me all through the journey. With hindsight, it was an experience of higher consciousness, which can only occur in the Now.

Third anecdote

This occurred about nine years ago. I was walking along the Ottawa River near our cottage practising breath-walking as a way to support myself in being mindful. It was early summer; the sky was clear blue, with some cotton clouds in the distance.

After about fifteen minutes of breath-walking, there was a shift in my perception, as though I had entered another reality. Everything around me appeared extraordinary. The leaves of a tree shimmering in the wind came alive, as though talking to me. The sky felt like an infinite body of God. There was a quickening of Spirit within me. The reflection of the sun's rays on the water sparkled like diamonds so beautiful as if I were seeing it for the very first time. I had entered into the eternal Now.

Most people have moments like this while watching a sunset or sunrise, playing with a child, being in nature, dancing, making love, or enjoying the company of friends or somebody they really like. In the beginning, you might not notice it, but sooner or later, there is bound to be a shift in your individual and collective consciousness. Humanity is on the verge of a quantum leap in the evolution of our consciousness. The eternal now is the gateway to our liberation from this collective matrix of the mind.

Obstacles to Being in the Now

Our only obstacle to being in the Now is our busy mind, which keeps us in the past or future. Our unconditioned consciousness is as vast as the sky. Mind or conditioned consciousness is like clouds and birds in this vast expanse of sky. Modern-day culture may seem like a grand conspiracy to keep the matrix of illusion alive by ensuring that people live and function predominantly in the egoic mode. At present, there is only a limited number of enlightened beings on the physical plane who have broken free of the matrix of mind. Most people have glimpses of this new reality. The possibility exists for all of us to break free.

Concentration, Awareness, and Mindfulness

As one practises being in the Now, the faculties of concentration, awareness, and mindfulness start to develop simultaneously in the individual. A good metaphor is to think of a photographer and his camera. *Concentration* allows him to focus like the zoom function of a camera. *Awareness* allows him to get a wide-angle view. *Mindfulness* is that moment-by-moment monitoring that assists him to maintain the camera steady.

Another metaphor is that of an eye surgeon. In order to perform laser surgery, he needs a focused laser beam (*concentration*). He needs a lens to look through (*awareness*). He also needs steady hands to perform the procedure (*mindfulness*).

How to Predictably Enter and Stay in the Now

Here are some of ideas that can be beneficial. Please do not feel obligated to practise all of them at once. Just work with one or two ideas; later, other suggestions can be explored.

1. Be regular with your daily spiritual practice (*sadhana*).

2. Give full attention to whatever you are doing.

3. Do one thing at a time when possible instead of always multitasking.

4. Create a day of mindfulness. If a day is not possible, then start with half a day.

5. Turn everyday routine activities such as washing dishes, going up a flight of stairs, eating, driving, etc., into a mindfulness practice.

6. Physical disciplines that promote mind-body connection can improve your ability to seize the moment. Yoga, Tai Chi, Chi Kung, martial arts, etc., when practised mindfully can improve your batting average of being present.

7. Since the mind by nature always wants to stay busy, give it something constructive to focus on such as breath, a mantra, an affirmation, or a daily spiritual thought.

8. Use every activity in your daily life for gathering Presence.

9. Stay grounded in your body awareness. Body is the elder brother of the mind. Body awareness calms down the restlessness of an active mind.

10. Fill your environment with pictures, artwork, and texts that keep bringing you back to the here and now.

11. Spend time in nature and practise walking meditation by synchronizing your steps with your breath.

12. Review and reread the material on the subjects of mindfulness and being in the Now.

13. Don't judge anything that is happening.

14. Accept all that is happening as though you have chosen it.

15. Pay attention to the silent gap between the sounds of the world. If there is a sound around you that you do not like, such as the noise of a lawn mower or of traffic, practise being transparent by letting it pass through you rather than resisting it.

16. If you hear a ringing sound or high-pitched "Eee" sound behind the ear, it could be the sound of silence. Try paying attention to it, since people only hear this sound when they are present in the moment.[13]

17. Use traffic lights and stop signs as a reminder to be present.

13　The sound of silence is different than tinnitus, which is the medical term for "hearing" noises in your ears when there is no outside source of the sounds. The noises you hear can be soft or loud. They may sound like ringing, blowing, roaring, buzzing, hissing, humming, whistling, or sizzling. Tinnitus can be very bothersome to the individual, whereas the sound of silence can be a great blessing to the seeker and an objective indication that he/she is present in this moment.

18. Have frequent three-minute breaks in the day to be silent or to pray. You could even do a three-minute meditation.

19. Use a chime or an alarm that is unobtrusive but can keep you mindful. I have found a simple vibrating device that can be set on a fifteen-minute repeat at regular or random intervals — a great way to gather presence throughout the day.

20. Sincerely pray for grace to show you the way to be present.

21. Choose hobbies and pastimes that promote presence over activities that cause mindlessness. Watch your habits regarding TV, Internet, and computer games. Use media creatively to help you to awaken. Use the mute button during commercials and practise being in the here and now.

22. Observe the devious ways of the ego within you without judging.

23. Create no psychological time by mentally dwelling on the past or future. It is okay to plan or make goals as long as you are living in the now. Sometimes planning is all that you need to do in this moment.

24. Have the patient attitude of a professional golfer who is not comparing his game with anybody but simply doing his best and over time dropping his handicap.

25. While conversing with people, keep a part of your attention on the body. Pay attention to the silence between the words.

26. Depending upon your religious bent, praying and practising the presence of God can be a very effective way to be in the here and now.

27. Avoid the use of chemicals or intoxicants that suppress the awareness of Now. If you take prescription drugs, periodically review them with your treating physician.

28. Go on a weekend retreat every one to three months.

29. Keep slowing down the churning of your mind by watching your breath or by repetition of God's name.

30. Create one or more periods of silence every day.

31. Try seeing the Divine in creation.

32. When upset, use it for awakening by being present.

～

Key Insights

1. Past and future are illusions. Now is all there is.
2. *Now* is the precious present, a gateway to our transformation and eventual liberation.
3. Our whole day can become a spiritual activity as we bring mindfulness into it.
4. If you can't feel joy and enthusiasm in what you are doing, try to reach for acceptance.
5. Develop consciousness roots in the body by being aware of the body sensations and the breath.

Questions to Reflect On

1. What is your relationship to the present moment? Do you usually accept it, resist it, or simply use it to get to some future moment?
2. Recall the times when you experienced the eternal now or felt very peaceful and joyful.
3. How could you improve your relationship with the present moment?

Awakening Practice (Walking Meditation)

The next time you go for a walk, turn it into a walking meditation. Breathe in to the count of three steps and breathe out to the count of three steps. Let all your senses come alive and have no judgments on anything you observe within or without. Feel the aliveness in the body. If possible, find a park bench and sit down for a few minutes to rest and observe the surroundings. Notice the growing presence in the body.

DEVELOPING
EMOTIONAL MATURITY

Growing old is mandatory; growing up is optional.

Vyasa

Chronological age ensures wrinkles but not emotional maturity. Education, especially higher education, is not necessarily an assurance that one will be emotionally mature. In fact, higher education may sometimes lead to lopsided development of intellect at the expense of the heart. My clients come from all walks of life. Among them are physicians, lawyers, scientists, teachers, university professors, CEOs, and regular folks. Some may come across as very bright and articulate individuals but often lag behind in their emotional development. It is very obvious in their choice of words — especially their limited emotional vocabulary — and the struggles they experience in their relationships with friends, families, colleagues, and in particular their intimate relationships. Often they behave like Mr. Spock, the Vulcan with the pointed ears, in the *Star Trek* series, who finds emotions illogical and difficult to grasp, as compared to Captain Kirk, who is very human and quite balanced and versatile in his usage of logic and emotions. Lack of emotional maturity seems to go hand in hand with unawareness or ego-based conditioned consciousness. Heaven consciousness cannot descend in our lives without a balanced development of head and heart.

What Is Emotional Maturity?

Emotional maturity implies the ability to be in touch with your feelings, the other person's feelings, and the context in which the emotions arise. The psychological term for this is *congruence* or *emotional intelligence*. Emotional maturity goes hand in hand with the evolution of awareness. An emotionally mature person has the ability to observe thoughts and feelings without identifying with them completely or putting them in the driver's seat. In psychological terms, emotional maturity has also been referred to as the emotional quotient (EQ).

Emotional and Intellectual Development

As a race, our emotional development has some catching up to do with our intellectual development. We are often untouched by the sufferings of our fellow human beings unless it is a close family member or someone we know. It is as though we suffer from emotional leprosy.[14]

Unless the intellect and emotions are integrated in a balanced way, the birth of Christ or Heaven consciousness cannot occur in us. Metaphysically speaking, unless Mary and Joseph marry, the child Jesus cannot be born. Here, Mary and Joseph represent the emotional and intellectual side and Jesus represents the awakened consciousness.

Even in Hindu scriptures such as the *Bhagavad-Gita*, there is reference to the notion of integrity in our thoughts, feelings, speech, and action as a desirable quality worth cultivating. The Sanskrit word for this state of integrity is *arjvam*. It is this congruent way of being that acts as fertile soil for the seeds of awakening to blossom. In his bestselling book, *Conversations with God*, the author, Neale Donald Walsh, asks God, "When will my life take off?" God replies, "When you think, feel, and act consistently."

Jesus was frequently asked about the Kingdom of Heaven and he used this parable to convey his teaching:

> The sower sows the seeds. Some seeds fall on the wayside, and birds come and eat them. Some fall on thorny ground, and the thorns don't allow the plants to flourish. Some fall on stony ground, and the heat of the sun scorches these seeds and they never get to germinate. And a few seeds fall on fertile soil and there is a one-hundredfold crop.

That is how the awakening or the Heaven consciousness grows in us when there is harmony between intellect, emotions, and action. It is like having a receptive and fertile soil of the body-mind field.

---

14 Leprosy is a medical condition in which the body loses sensitivity to pain and temperature. The end result is tissue damage and disfigured hands, feet, and face.

Neuroanatomy and Emotional Development

From a neuroanatomical point of view, we have three brains, *the visceral brain, the emotional brain, and the intellectual brain or neocortex.* One simple way to conceptualize it is to imagine a stick as the spinal cord and brain stem, representing the visceral brain. On top of that is sitting an egg, which is the middle brain, and it represents the limbic system or emotional brain. Over the egg is a helmet, which is the neocortex or intellectual brain. The visceral brain and the emotional brain are very closely integrated, but the neocortex is still evolving and has not completely integrated with the other two brains.

The process of emotional maturity involves the evolution of awareness, the development of emotional vocabulary, and integration of our thinking brain with the emotional and visceral brain areas. Young children are still developing emotional vocabulary. They usually express themselves as either feeing good or bad. Often many of my intellectual clients either avoid using emotional language and start every sentence with "I think" or limit themselves to a few common and safe expressions such as, "interesting" . . . "fascinating" . . . "brilliant." It takes emotional maturity to not only experience a whole range of emotions, but also to express them constructively and non-violently and have the language to identify the finer shades of anger, sadness, fear, guilt, regret, and even positive emotions. Emotional maturity also involves mind-body integration and the presence to observe the procession of thoughts, images, feelings, and body sensations without getting caught up in them.

Another significant area of the brain that evolves with maturity is the prefrontal cortex, which has also been referred to as the CEO of our brain. The human brain has over 100 billion neurons — the approximate number of all the stars and planets. Our brain is *plastic*, which means it is changeable; there are always new neuronal pathways being created. People who are emotionally mature and integrated have a higher degree of brain-wave *coherence*. Coherence is a term used to describe the degree of synchronization among the neurons of the two brain areas, not unlike what a conductor of an orchestra creates among musicians playing different instruments. As we practise daily spiritual discipline and learn from life experiences, our prefrontal cortex (CEO) also matures and develops extensive networking with other parts of the brain. On the other hand, drug and alcohol abuse, the side-effects of certain prescription drugs, stress, neurological conditions, and trauma can hinder the evolution of the prefrontal cortex.

Proper Attitudes toward Emotions

It is human to have emotions and feelings. Emotions are neither good nor bad, right nor wrong. They are an integral part of our feedback system, a kind of internal GPS; or akin to signals on the dashboard of our car. Often people avoid facing their feelings or even acknowledging them and, in the process, create a backlog of unprocessed feelings. They may use a variety of coping mechanisms, such as suppression, denial, blaming, rationalization, or glossing over with spirituality while seething with anger underneath their peaceful facade, distracting themselves, and indulging in food or other addictive substances. It is not uncommon for people to displace their anger toward one person onto another. The unintegrated, suppressed, and unresolved emotions act as dark clouds that veil the light of our being.

These clouds veil the love, peace, and joy that we all want to experience and are looking for directly or indirectly — not knowing that what we are seeking is essentially the very nature of our being.

During my formative years, I grew up in a home where my father used either logic or a blaming response to cope with life stresses. My mother coped by being a placator and, in the process, often denied herself while caring for others. I found myself using all three coping responses. Four years of personal psychoanalysis with two different analysts offered me an opportunity to explore my feelings, perceptions, beliefs, expectations, and deeper universal yearnings of love, peace, joy, spiritual evolution, making a contribution, and reaching my full potential. It helped to have a more balanced development of head and heart. It was near the end of psychoanalysis that I started my spiritual quest. After a course of successful psychotherapy, people are generally ready to start their spiritual quest. Since the conclusion of my psychoanalysis, I have been consciously integrating emotions through emotional awareness meditations, clearing letters, journalling, personal growth workshops, and mindfulness meditations. This is emotional hygiene and is a vital part of self-care and daily spiritual practice.

Integrating the neocortex with the other two brain areas is a gradual evolutionary process that requires a conscious development of emotional maturity.

We need to use every upset as an opportunity for awakening. An upset brings us to a crossroad, and if we process it mindfully, then we can learn the lesson, grow in wisdom, and mature. The process of upset brings something from the basement (unconscious) to the main floor (conscious), and now there is an opportunity for us to observe it, integrate it, and let go of that which no longer serves us. Emotional maturity goes hand in hand with the degree of happiness and experience of success and fulfillment in our lives.

Practising Emotional Awareness in Relationships

The most helpful thing we can do for someone who is upset is to offer him or her some emotional air by listening empathically. I often say to my clients that when somebody is upset, he needs an ear, a heart, and a touch — not an intellectual response. Offering logic to somebody who is upset is like serving him a bag of salt when he is thirsty and asking for water. It would invariably get him more frustrated and not understood; and you may be seen as an opponent.

An effective way to calm somebody who is very upset is through "*Poffing*" her.[15] Here, the "P" stands for paraphrasing what she is expressing, "O" for okay to her feelings, and "F" for offering language to her feelings. Most people can learn to use it with some practice. *It is important not to take somebody's upset personally but rather touch it with the gentle hands of loving kindness, remembering that all upsets are essentially a call for love.* Once the person has calmed down, then he or she may be ready for a more rational approach.

A clearing letter is another effective way to process thoughts and feelings. The next time you are bothered by strong emotions, try emptying out all of your thoughts and feeling in a clearing letter and then shred or burn the paper, depending on what is suitable. Often this is enough to clear the emotional backlog, and forgiveness may occur naturally. Sometimes a course of psychotherapy may be needed to facilitate healing and emotional maturity. Integration of emotions is necessary not only to deal with negative emotions but

15   Sincere acknowledgement to Ken Keyes for his teachings on pathways to higher consciousness.

also to deal with our passions, lust, and strong desires, which can complicate our lives if allowed free rein.

Emotional awareness meditation is another practical and effective way to integrate emotions through witnessing them. It is like being as still as a mountain while facing strong emotional winds.

Here are a couple of examples from my clinical practice that may illustrate the value of integrating emotions rather than acting them out or suppressing them.

> Ann was very attracted to her husband's best friend and was overwhelmed by her thoughts and feelings. She was afraid that she would end up having an affair. I taught her the emotional awareness process of learning to witness the emotions and not judge them but simply be present. Some psychotherapeutic support along with the practice of this meditation offered her a way to process those strong emotions without acting them out or breaking her friendship.

> Joyce was ready to give up her very high position as a government employee because of her inability to resolve conflicts with her boss. She was not interested in psychotherapy and arrived at the session with a resignation letter prepared. I provided her with an outline of the clearing letter, with the simple instruction to try the process. I encouraged her to wait for a few more weeks before submitting her resignation. She made copies of the letter and whenever she was upset, she would fire off a clearing letter and shred it rather than stewing in her unexpressed feelings. Within a month's time, she felt much more comfortable and at ease with her emotions. She was able to express herself appropriately and deal with the conflict with her boss in a rather constructive way. The effectiveness of this process inspired her to come back for some further psychotherapeutic work. The good news is that she did not need to resign from her job and even got a promotion because of her mature approach to the interpersonal challenges.

Emotional Maturity in Politics

We all recognize the importance of having emotionally mature leaders. It is easier to connect with leaders who are comfortable with their emotions. Examples of such leaders are Pierre Trudeau,

John F. Kennedy, Martin Luther King, Nelson Mandela, the Dalai Lama, Mahatma Gandhi, and Barack Obama.

To resolve world issues, to understand each other and have a constructive dialogue, we need awakened leaders who are emotionally mature and capable of empathy; we need those who can tolerate a different point of view, use differences as an opportunity for enrichment, and appreciate the unity in diversity.

Emotions as Guidance System

A plane from New York to Los Angeles does not fly in a straight line; it usually zigzags. The guidance system within the plane keeps making course corrections, and the plane eventually lands at the desired destination. Similarly, our emotions are an integral part of our guidance system. Positive emotions indicate that we are moving toward our desired goal, and negative emotions indicate that we are in resistance mode and we need to realign.

Grounding Emotions

We are a living matrix, and emotional energy flows through us like a river. Any obstruction to the flow creates a dam, and tension builds up in the body-mind matrix. Allowing the flow to occur unhampered is the objective of the practice of grounding emotions. A healer friend of mine has a unique talent in grounding, and his insight is that if you take longer than ninety seconds to ground an emotion, it indicates resistance, and you need more practice. At an energetic level, our emotions are nothing but the same universal divine energy, or *Shakti*, coming to us wearing different masks.

Key Insights

1. As a race, we need to cultivate EQ, or emotional maturity. Growing old in years or education is not an assurance of emotional maturity.

2. Developing emotional maturity is a spiritual practice. Some personal growth work through clearing letters, emotional awareness meditation, and psychotherapy can be a valuable aid in integrating a backlog of unsorted feelings.

3. Integration of emotions and intellect creates a fertile soil for the seeds of awakening to germinate.

4. Emotions are not good or bad but are feedback from our guidance system. Emotions are energy in motion, and we can learn to integrate this energy promptly through grounding.

5. Emotional maturity goes hand in hand with degree of happiness, success, and fulfillment.

Questions to Reflect On

1. How do you deal with stressful emotions? Do you suppress your feelings, blame somebody, think your way out of it, or distract yourself with food, drink, TV, media, or an activity?

2. How do you deal with conflicts in your intimate relationships?

3. How were emotions handled in your family of origin?

Awakening Practice
(Emotional Awareness Meditation)

Emotional awareness meditation is not only a way to integrate emotions but also a very effective way to connect with the source. It is like following a ray of sunshine back to the sun. In order to be able to practise this meditation, it is important that you have been cultivating mindfulness. Without the energy of mindfulness, it is difficult to observe your feelings and not be swayed by them.

Sit comfortably and ensure you won't be distracted. Now breathe mindfully for a couple of minutes by following your breath. Mentally say, "Breathing in, I am aware" during inhalation and, "Breathing out, I am aware" during exhalation. Only when you feel established in the mindfulness of your breath, turn your attention toward your feelings. If there is any feeling such as anger, sadness, or even lust, you can mentally say, "Breathing in, I am aware of my sadness," "Breathing out, I take care of my sadness." Treat your feelings with kindness and compassion, as though they were little children who need your love, acceptance, and attention. Observe the magic of transformation and healing.

DISSOLVING PAIN AND SUFFERING

All is suffering.
Gautama Buddha

The Anatomy of Emotional Pain

After his enlightenment, Buddha taught the four noble truths; the first was, *"All is suffering."* He was perhaps referring to the basic unsatisfactory nature of life that is subject to change, illness, accidents, old age, and death. The same truth is echoed in the other religious and spiritual traditions. Seers and enlightened masters from the Yoga tradition have boldly stated, *"Sarvam Dhukham,"* meaning, "everybody suffers." Guru Nanak, an enlightened master from the Sikh tradition, also said it poetically: *"Nanak dhukia sab sansar,"* meaning that everybody in the whole world is suffering. Henry David Thoreau, an American philosopher, confirmed this insight in his statement, "The mass of men lead lives of quiet desperation." My intention is not to dishearten the reader but to accurately diagnose the human condition and point toward a way out of this inevitable suffering suggested by the masters from different wisdom traditions.

While pain is inevitable, suffering—which is a reaction to the pain—is optional. Our body and mind accumulate some degree of residual pain long after the original incidents have passed, unless we are already evolved and can transmute the base metal of suffering into the gold of joy. This residual pain that accumulates over time in our mind and body feels like a trapped energy and behaves like an entity referred to as the pain body by Eckhart Tolle.

It is almost like being infested with an alien parasite that lives in us, has its own energetic frequency, attracts further negativity, and tries to avoid the light of awareness. The pain body's main purpose is to live on and it accomplishes that by clouding our awareness and keeping painful memories of the past alive; in the process, the ego is strengthened. The pain body may be dormant in most people, being triggered only occasionally by a life situation or a person. In other people, it may be active more often than not. Some people are so caught up in their victim story that their very identity has become either a "victim" or a "survivor." These people are often very unhappy, and unless you are highly aware while interacting with them, it is easy to get dragged down by their negativity. Sometimes a course of psychotherapy can awaken a dormant pain body, as evident in the following example.

> Richard, a single salesman in his forties, related to me that he seemed to be doing okay until he started a course of intensive analytic psychotherapy in order to work out his relationship issues with the opposite sex. Now he is anxious most of the time, cannot sleep well, and is frequently bothered by disturbing dreams. He wondered if he had opened a Pandora's Box by his overzealous attempts to engage in intensive therapy without having the infrastructure of a balanced life and a spiritual practice. Therapy, instead of liberating him, had awakened his pain body, and the troublesome symptoms, if untreated, could lead to an illness.

When working with a client who has a heavy pain body, the therapist needs to be highly aware, no longer subject to egoic mind dominance, and versatile in different therapeutic modalities. People who hurt themselves or others are in the grip of a pain body that has been activated; it has temporarily taken over their faculty of judgment.

When the pain body becomes active, the person can behave either as a perpetrator or a victim. In the ultimate sense, there is not much difference between the two roles. In the beginning of a new relationship, things may be fine, and then in a year or so, when the couple has already tied the knot, the pain body of one of the partners starts to wake up and show its ugly head, and then the fun begins. When that happens, people often wonder if they are with the wrong person and have made a terrible mistake when they see their partner behaving inappropriately while under the influence of the pain body. All relationships are designed to help us grow in awareness, and part of the process of growth is to bring to surface all that is unconscious.

It is helpful to remember that relationships are here simply to help us grow in unconditional love and awareness. Relationships, especially intimate relationships, are a school for awakening and not the Hollywood version of "happily ever after." Our main and only assignment is to forgive ourselves and everybody else in our lives so that we can learn our lessons and grow in our experience of love.

When somebody's pain body is active, the person finds it hard to tolerate another person's joy. He may sulk, be angry, attack, defend, or even hurt himself. Clinically, I have observed that people who cope by "placating" often hurt themselves, while those with a "blaming" coping stance may attack someone else when experiencing emotional pain. Often the person in the grip of the pain body radiates a negative field of energy, and you can notice it in the facial expression, glazed look in the eyes, or an uncomfortable feeling in your own body when interacting with him.

Energetically, the pain body is trapped life force and needs to be integrated. But if you are not very aware, it is easy to get entangled in an argument or some kind of drama with a partner in the grip of an active pain body. Eventually, this could bring both partners down into a lower vibration of consciousness and thereby perpetuate the karmic cycle of sufferings. Often the pain body can resonate with the pain body of other people and create a collective pain body. It is the collective pain body that is the cause of conflicts between nations, riots, terrorism, and wars. Many victims of a tragedy, or those with strong ideological issues, etc., might find their individual pain body reinforced by the collective pain body of the group. This can find an aggressive expression inwardly or outwardly. Related presentations by the media, movies, museums, historical writings, and politicians may all keep the pain body energized.

Since the pain body wants to stay alive, it uses many ways to keep the person in unawareness. People often distract themselves in various ways or get into unconscious addictive behaviours such as drinking, smoking, drugs, sex, etc., to soothe themselves; nevertheless, the pain body continues to live on.

However, the pain body cannot live for long in the light of presence—just as night disappears when the sun rises.

Recently, at a retreat, I met a Buddhist lama who happened to visit my hometown of Amritsar. He was very impressed by the Golden Temple, its beauty and sacredness; then there was an expression of pain on his face when he described what he had seen in the Sikh museum. He was referring to the paintings depicting horrible atrocities done to the Sikhs.

While it is important to learn from the past, and history is very valuable, perhaps some of our attempts to preserve history contribute to the karmic cycle of pain, especially if the light of awareness in the individual is not strong enough to look at the pain without being distressed by it. If a Buddhist lama could not look at pain without being troubled by it, imagine what a challenge it could be for us.

Psychotherapy as a discipline can be very helpful in dissolving pain. Although, in the case of Richard, the process of inappropriate therapy apparently did more harm than good. I promote the development of a degree of awareness in the clients and a firm foundation of therapeutic alliance with me as their therapist before exploring their deeper issues.

Buddhist meditation teachers have a similar insight: Before somebody begins insight meditation (*Vipassana*), which involves looking at all that shows up, including stored pain, first and foremost he/she needs to develop concentration through *Samatha* practice, which would allow him/her to be stable like a mountain when faced with the stormy winds of an awakening pain body.

Generally, as the pain body is starting to awaken, there are some early warning signs. It could be in the form of negativity, a sombre mood, a need for some drama in a relationship, or some unconscious self-sabotage behaviour. The anguish people feel when they are in the grip of their pain body is due to their experience of being cut off from Source. Outwardly, they may attack the people around them or punish themselves in some way. Yet at a spiritual level, they are in pain and are really calling out for love and healing. The people around them may take their negativity personally and react.

How to Dissolve the Pain Body

Cultivate witness consciousness
Witness consciousness is a non-judgmental observation of thoughts and feelings that interrupts the process of identification. Witness

consciousness is like being able to sit on the balcony of your awareness and watch the procession of thoughts, feelings, and body sensations pass by. Meditation, mindfulness practice, and prayer can help in the cultivation of witness consciousness.

I often teach my clients to observe their pain body during our session so that they can watch it diminish right in front of their eyes. This is very reassuring for them and they can begin to realize that they are not their thoughts and feelings but rather Awareness itself.

Interrupt the pattern

Especially if the person's presence is not very strong, when the pain body surfaces, it is sometimes okay to consciously interrupt it by using constructive distractions rather than wallowing in the pain.

A client of mine, whenever in acute pain, found that she could interrupt it by playing gospel music. In my own experience, one time there was a family conflict starting to emerge, and suddenly my wife suggested that we chant "Om." Surprisingly, everybody agreed. After just a few chants, we all felt a shift in our consciousness and were able to resume the dialogue in a productive manner. It was as though the chanting had stopped the negative process in its tracks.

For some people, exercise, doing jumping jacks, or chanting loudly can be ways to interrupt the pattern until the person has developed enough presence to dissolve it through witnessing it. Interrupting the pain body is akin to taking a CD and putting scratches on it so that it does not play again easily.

Look for the payoff

Unconscious payoff can keep the pain body alive indefinitely. Victim identity is one such payoff. Many well-meaning support groups can keep the identity of being a victim alive by reinforcing it. An unsettled compensation case or an unresolved insurance or disability claim may directly or indirectly keep the pain body alive. Further, the disability claim process often keeps the person stuck in pain by frequent requests for information by the insurance companies, having to see different specialists, talk about their problems over and over again, having to justify their suffering, and experiencing frequent delays in getting a prompt response. All of this keeps the memory of pain alive and actually worsens the clinical outcome. My intention is to raise awareness and support a reform in the disability process but in no way deny or minimize the genuine suffering of all those people on disability.

Practise forgiveness of self and others

One of the most significant components of healing is to forgive so as to remove blockages to the flow of love. The majority of my clients and many of my colleagues are confused about forgiveness. Forgiveness is a process of "mental hygiene." It is something we need to do every day and whenever we feel that our mind is contaminated with negativity. Forgiveness and compassion happen naturally when we are in a state of grace, another name for presence. We may even realize that there are no victims and no perpetrators, only volunteers in the classroom of life designed to help us grow and evolve in our consciousness. (The forgiveness process is explored in detail in the next chapter.)

Aspire consciously

Aspiration (the soul's cry for grace) burns away all impurities and imperfections. When we aspire, we feel hope, gratitude, and a feeling of being connected with Source. The aspiration flame is that torch of ascending consciousness that needs to be kept burning. Demands of ordinary living and everyday negativity can smother this flame. Daily spiritual practice keeps stoking the fire. Aspiration raises our vibrational frequency, and all that no longer serves us falls away. It is like the sonic toothbrush that controls plaque by causing the tooth to vibrate at a frequency higher than that of the plaque.

Loving-kindness meditation

This is a very effective way to soothe pain and at the same time cultivate compassion and open the fountain of love and aspiration. It also offers protection from the little me / ego self. The Pali word for loving-kindness practice is *metta*, which means "friendliness."

> Bob was a middle-aged client who came to see me very
> distressed due to an unresolved workmen's compensation case.
> He had a lot of anger, bitterness, and resentment toward many
> people. In my brief intervention, I coached him on emotional

hygiene, forgiveness, and loving kindness. After a few sessions, he stopped coming. A few years later, he called me and asked me to see his son. During this meeting, he informed me that our few sessions and the practice of loving-kindness meditation had been most helpful to him in dissolving bitterness and bringing him to a peaceful state whereby he was able to resolve his dispute in a win-win way.

The loving-kindness meditation is described at the end of this chapter.

To sum up some of the ways of dissolving pain, I have made an acronym of the word.

P. *Presence/awareness. Cultivate it.*

A. *Aspiration and acceptance. Accept what is and aspire at every moment.*

I. *Insight. Practise looking at the pain without judgment and regard it as a teacher. Pain is like darkness and cannot stand the presence of light.*

N. *Now. Being in the now is a spiritual discipline of transmuting pain into* Consciousness.

Dissolving Collective Pain

As we can start to dissolve individual pain, it becomes easier to participate in group rituals or group activities to dissolve the pain of our neighbours, friends, and community. Whenever a group of people gets together to perform a ritual of meditation or some ceremony, it is bound to influence the vibrational level of the whole community. The TM organization has often done studies demonstrating that whenever there is a TM event occurring in a city, and a couple of thousand meditators are meditating, during that period there is a significant drop in the crime rate. All traditions have beautiful rituals that can be utilized to create a healing vibrational energy on the planet.

The work of Dr. Massuro Emoto on water crystals is very inspiring. Even a simple prayer for an hour by Rev. Kato (mentioned in Dr. Emoto's first book on water crystals, titled *Messages from Water*) could change the water crystals in a polluted lake at Fujiwara Dam in Japan. Imagine a million people praying every day at the same time for planetary healing. What a profound impact it could have!

James Tyman's work with Emissary of Light is another example of emissaries who would sit around in a circle with the intention to bring down light for the planet. All spiritual circles that are operating in integrity are creating a vibrational grid to usher in Heaven.

It is very important to remember that our healing is intertwined, and there is no individual salvation. However, charity begins at home, and one needs to start working on one's personal growth and healing before attempting to dissolve the collective pain of the world.

Key Insights

1. Everybody, sooner or later, suffers in some form or other.

2. The residual pain that accumulates in the body-mind field over time may create a pain body that behaves almost like an alien.

3. Before looking at pain deeply, it is important that the person has cultivated some presence through mindfulness.

4. The pain body cannot live for long in the light of presence.

5. Forgiveness of self and others can help heal us as individuals and collectively, our relationships, and the planet.

Questions to Reflect On

1. How do you cope with upsetting emotions?

2. How mindful are you these days?

3. Remember the last time your pain body was triggered and notice how you handled it.

Awakening Practice (Loving Kindness Meditation)

Take a comfortable posture and breathe mindfully for a few minutes. Once you notice yourself feeling calmer, start repeating the following affirmations silently. You can prayerfully modify or create new affirmations to meet your changing needs.

May I be free from pain and suffering.

May I be happy and healthy.

May I live and grow in love and compassion.

May I be prosperous.

May I awaken to my full potential and be liberated.

Initially, you may focus only on yourself and your loved ones but, as you become established in your mindfulness practice, you may find it easier to send love even to difficult persons. All you need to do is replace "I" with "you" in the affirmations. In addition to yourself, you can eventually include people from the following categories:

Benefactors

A mentor or a guru

Grandparents and other ancestors

Parents

Immediate family members

Friends

Relatives

Neutral persons

Difficult persons

All beings

LEARNING TO FORGIVE

Forgiveness is my function as the light of the world.
A Course in Miracles

This is a subject fraught with confusion, misunderstanding, and lack of agreement among the experts in the field. Furthermore, nowhere in my psychiatric training or in my four years of psychoanalysis was there any meaningful discussion on the subject of forgiveness. Only when I started to evolve spiritually did I realize the truth in the above statement that forgiveness is my function as the light of the world. In the Hindu tradition, forgiveness is described as the greatest action (*dharma*) in the Sanskrit saying, "*Kshma Parmo dharma.*" We have all heard the expression "*To err is human, to forgive divine.*" Even Jesus talked to his disciples about the value of forgiving one's enemies and even praying for them.

The question that naturally arises is, "What is forgiveness?"

Definition of Forgiveness

The simplest definition is that it is a hygienic act. Just like physical or dental hygiene, there is also mental hygiene. If you don't brush your teeth, your mouth will taste bad. If you do not forgive, your mind will be contaminated with residual negative emotions which will only attract more suffering. Forgiveness, therefore, is gift of love that you give to yourself. The forgiveness process involves a willingness to see the situation through the loving eyes of the spirit, rather than through the fragmented and distorted perception of the egoic consciousness.

Why Do We Need to Forgive?

By forgiving, you are setting yourself free from the self-created prison of *sin, separation, and fear* in its various expressions. By not forgiving, you are really the one who is suffering. Imagine holding a burning coal in your hand; before you can throw it away, it has already burnt holes through the skin of your hand. Similarly, all of our negative emotions are already causing a toxic violence to our system. In my practice, I have repeatedly observed lack of forgiveness to be at the core of many physical and emotional ailments. We need to forgive because we believe that sin is real, and in our separation consciousness we see a victim and a persecutor. We need to forgive because we cannot just forget it and move on. If there were a way for us to selectively forget certain negative experiences, just like deleting files from our computer, then perhaps there would be no need for forgiveness.

We are supposed to remember our experiences so that we can reflect on them, learn from the past, and evolve. Frequent forgetfulness can be a cause for concern regarding the possibility of an underlying medical problem. *When the forgiveness process is complete, you may still remember the incident, but the emotional charge is not there.*

Yet another benefit of forgiveness is that it acts like a soothing balm for our hurt and grievances. Resentment — which is a lack of forgiveness — clouds our perception and taints our glasses, and we look at the world with jaundiced eyes. We end up projecting our negativity onto others and even develop blind spots, as evident in this example.

> Cheryl is a young Caucasian woman in her early forties who came from an alcoholic background. Despite her participation in Al-Anon and her disdain for alcoholism, she still ended up attracting a series of partners all of whom had drinking problems. Only after she was able to forgive herself and her past did her relationship pattern begin to change.

Forgiveness, therefore, is the detergent that cleans our perception glasses. Imagine how unsafe it would be to move about in the world with perception glasses that are tainted by resentment and therefore not being able to see the world as it is.

Misconceptions about Forgiveness

People often have many misconceptions about forgiveness. I have attempted to respond to the ones that come up frequently during the therapeutic encounter.

1. *Does forgiveness mean that I have to condone somebody's actions?*
Forgiveness does not mean you have to find excuses for somebody's behaviour. If you are hurt, you need to acknowledge it. You need to forgive because you want to be happy and free. It is not the snakebite that kills but the circulation of the venom. When we relive the painful memory in our mind, we are re-traumatizing ourselves again and again.

2. *Does forgiveness mean I have to rationalize or deny my feelings?*
The first step to forgiveness is to acknowledge your feelings and give yourself some psychological air. Acknowledging your feelings does not mean enshrining them and making a mausoleum of a story around it. Just as an abscess does not heal until the pus is discharged, similarly we need to empty out our suppressed negative emotions in a constructive way before we can be ready to forgive.

3. *Does forgiveness mean I have to turn the other cheek and allow myself to be abused again?*
No. Forgiveness does not mean you have to allow yourself to be abused. However, in the unhealed consciousness of the ego, we are likely to keep recreating the cycle of violence in our lives. Turning the other cheek is a practice that happens naturally when you are in a state of Grace, where, like a mother, you see the other person's anger as a call for love from a child. One cannot fake that state of Grace.

4. *Does forgiveness mean that I have to contact the person or invite him/her back into my life?*
No. You do not need to contact or invite somebody back in your life if that is not appropriate. Forgiveness is still possible even if the person is dead. Sometimes, in the process of forgiveness, the healing is so complete and profound that there is mutual reconciliation, which may be in the highest interest of all.

5. *Does forgiveness mean the other person can get away with murder?*
No. Forgiveness is happening inside your mind and *you* are the one who is being set free. If guided by your Higher Self, you could even fire somebody for incompetence, yet be at peace

in your heart. It would show in your language, your nonverbal communication, and the peaceful manner in which you let him/her go.

Similarly, you could even sue someone or go to war and still be at peace in your heart. As a child, I was quite fascinated by the artefacts in the Sikh museum, housed in the famous Golden Temple. The museum still has the arrows of *Shri Guru Gobind Singh*, the tenth guru of the Sikhs (December 22, 1666–October 7, 1708). He was a saint, a poet, a great king, and a brave warrior. All of his arrows had gold at the base. Even though he had to fight the unrighteous Muslim king, Aurangzeb, in his heart he had a deep compassion for the soldiers who would be wounded. The gold was meant to financially assist the wounded to get proper care.

6. *Does forgiveness occur the first time?*
   In some instances, there is such a dramatic transformation that forgiveness may happen in a single session. More often than not, forgiveness happens in stages. The ongoing practice of forgiveness is like chipping away at a granite stone until it disappears completely. Forgiveness is like taking a shower: We don't just take it once; it is an ongoing act of daily self-care.

The Forgiveness Process[16]

Forgiveness is an internal process that allows us to reconnect with our Higher Self. When successful, it leads to peace, joy, love, gratitude, and freedom. There is a general sense of well-being and acceptance. One lets go of the intense emotions around the hurt. There is no longer any need for past pain; no longer any need to punish. During psychotherapy, clients often experience forgiveness. Their healing process usually includes the following steps:

- Acknowledging the hurt
- Experientially exploring the feelings around the hurt
- No longer playing the victim
- Changing the perception of the hurt

---

16 My sincere acknowledgements to Dr. John Banmen and Kathlyne Maki–Banmen, my mentors in the *Satir Model* for their teachings on "The Forgiveness Process" and the recent studies on forgiveness.

- Learning from the past
- Beginning to live in the present

Instead of forgiving, we might:

- Deny
- Ignore
- Blame others
- Blame ourselves
- Be a victim
- Choose anger
- Be a "survivor"

Often people are so upset that they are not ready to forgive. My usual response is: "I understand that you are not ready to forgive. You can choose to suffer, since it is your life after all. But for how long do you want to keep suffering? Have you not already suffered enough?"

This would usually give them cause to think and embrace the letting go process. People often wonder if forgiveness is for the meek and the weak. *Actually, it takes strength of character to choose to forgive.*

Recent studies reveal that forgiveness leads to:

- Fewer health problems
- Reduced heart disease
- Less stress
- Beneficial impact on blood pressure, muscle tension, and immune response

Once people are convinced of the urgent need for forgiveness, the next question that usually follows is, "So how do I forgive?"

In response to this question, here is a buffet of options to choose from.

Different ways to forgive

1. *Prayer and meditation*
   For those who can pray and meditate, this may be the simplest process to invoke the Higher Self. A sincere willingness to see another way is all that may be needed to embark on the

process. Prayer and meditation go hand in hand and are like flip sides of the same coin.

2. *Confession/Reconciliation*
For some of my Catholic clients, a regular confession and attending a weekly mass may keep them in a state of Grace. Many of my Catholic clients are non-practising and would rather deal with the issue of forgiveness in a psychotherapeutic setting. Sometimes, full expressions of feelings might not be possible in the confession process.

3. *Mindfulness practice*
Mindfulness practice is a very potent antidote to human suffering. As we practise being in the here and now and witness our thoughts and emotions, the identification with the content of mind is broken, often leading to a shift in perception and a feeling of freedom. Giving full attention to whatever you are doing can be a very practical way to cultivate mindfulness. If you are eating, eat mindfully and savour every bite. If you are washing dishes, then turn that activity into a practice: feel the warmth of the water, smell the soap, and let that activity be an experience of the sacred. Mindfulness, though it traces its source to Buddhism, has found its way into mainstream clinical practice. There are several indexed scientific studies that lend credence to its therapeutic value.

4. *Clearing letter*
This may seem like a simple tool, yet it can be very transformative. All you need is a pen and paper and some quiet space where you won't be interrupted for the next half hour or so. You just write an uncensored letter to the person you are upset with and pour out all your feelings on paper. It does not matter if your upset happens to be with God — the process is still the same.

Once you have expressed all your feelings on paper, write yourself back a response, the kind of apology letter you would like to receive, if that were ever possible. Now read this letter only once, attentively, and then immediately shred it, burn it in your fireplace, or simply tear it into small pieces and throw it into the garbage. Please don't mail these letters or keep them around. These letters have a tendency of getting into the wrong hands. Also, by reading it more than once, you will only be recycling emotional garbage. The process of shredding or burning is a ritual that our mind likes.

It may take three or four letters before you may feel some relief. Once you are at peace, that may be the time to write an actual letter to the other person that you could mail if you choose to, since you are now more likely to be constructive and balanced in your outlook, and this kind of non-violent communication promotes better relationships and healing. I have countless examples of how this simple tool has been so very effective in the forgiveness process.

5. *Psychotherapy*
Psychotherapy can be a very legitimate way to promote healing and spiritual growth. As you already know, my own spiritual quest started after a period of psychoanalysis, which is a form of intensive psychotherapy. There are over 250 kinds of psychotherapies and they all have some common elements that make them effective, such as a trusting alliance, unconditional regard, confidentiality, and an experiential component, all facilitated by the warm personality of the therapist. Beneficial results tend to be the evolution of awareness, acceptance, and a shift in perception.

Most therapists combine different techniques, drawing on their own life experience. Finding a suitable therapist may require some shopping to find a match between your needs and the therapist's expertise. There are some therapeutic techniques such as EMDR (eye movement desensitization reprocessing) and thought field therapy that have claimed effectiveness in dealing with significant traumas. Not all therapists consciously utilize forgiveness rituals in their approach.

6. *Guided visual imagery*
Some people are better at visualizing than others. There are excellent audio recordings available that can allow us to use visualization as a way to forgive and heal ourselves physically, emotionally, and spiritually. One of my teachers, Brandon Bays, the author of the *Journey* book, healed herself of a tumour by practising a form of visualization and introspection. A journey process allows you to connect with the Higher Self / Source, empty out all emotions, release cell

memories, and put the balm of forgiveness on the wounds.

You could practise a journey with the help of a Brandon Bays CD or with the assistance of a trained journey practitioner. Louise Hay, in her book, *You Can Heal Your Life*,[17] has offered her insights on the forgiveness process. She also has many CDs with guided imagery on forgiveness.

7. *Therapeutic ritual*
Our mind likes rituals and can benefit from them. There are a couple of rituals that I have adopted into my practice. The first one is a simple ritual of *"emptying out,"* which allows somebody who is very upset to express all his thoughts and feelings toward another person without being interrupted. I may use an empty chair or have him talk to me while pretending that I am the other person. My role is to hold the sacred space and listen while prompting him to keep emptying out by simple statements such as, "Thank you. What else?"

This process I initially learned in the context of a Gestalt therapy workshop and also subsequently in a "Healing with Conscious Communication" workshop as a part of my journey practitioner's program offered by Journey USA.

The other ritual is to have the person complete the following sentence as many times as she may need in a particular session:

*The person I need to forgive is_____
for_____.*

My response is, *"Thank you. I set you free."*

By saying, "Thank you. I set you free," I am simply reminding the person that he/she is the one who is being set free in the forgiveness process.

Here I acknowledge the teachings of Louise Hay, from whom I first learned this process; since then, I have adopted it with good results.

8. *Vasna daha tantra*
Vasna means thoughts and feelings, *daha* is a verb for offering

---

17   Louise Hay, *You Can Heal Your Life* (Carson, CA: Hay House, Inc., 1994).

to fire, and the word *tantra* means a ritual. This is an ancient
ritual from tantra yoga whereby you write on a piece of paper
or a thin wooden parchment all that you need to forgive or any
tendencies that you need to let go and offer it to the fire in a
prayerful way. *Tantra* suggests that our basic nature is whole
and complete, and all we need to do is some periodic internal
cleaning so that the sun of our radiant Self can shine again.
People are often concerned about the safety of making an open
fire indoors, especially if they don't have a fireplace. One can
improvise by using a shredder or by cutting it into very small
pieces and releasing it.

9. *Healing stream ritual*
   This ritual is an adaptation to the above practice, especially
   if you are in nature and close to a river or a flowing body of
   water. In order to practise this, you need to gather a pile of dry
   leaves. Then find a quiet spot near the river to sit. Now think
   of something you need to release or forgive, imagine placing it
   on a leaf, and mindfully place it into the river. Keep repeating
   this process until you have nothing more to release or are out
   of leaves. Now look at this trail of leaves flowing away from
   you and notice the peace and silence growing within you. You
   may sit in silence or meditate for a few more minutes.

10. *Pratipaksha bhavna*
    This is a Sanskrit expression for "balanced perception." The
    process involves consciously focusing on the positive qualities
    of the person that you are upset with. Sometimes I might give
    my clients homework to do whereby they have to come up with
    at least twenty-five good qualities about the other person and
    themselves. This could be a very transformative practice and
    invariably leads to balanced perception.

11. *Grounding practice*
    Thoughts and feelings have an energy that is palpable. Non-
    forgiveness and non-acceptance feel like a block or resistance
    to the flow of life energy. Grounding is a form of mindfulness
    practice whereby you allow the energy to flow through you as
    though you were transparent. Alternatively, you could imagine
    standing under a waterfall and let it wash you both outside
    and inside and imagine your feet have roots in the earth. This

process requires some practice and is easier to do if you have been meditating regularly.

The above list of eleven techniques does not represent all of the possible ways to connect with our Source through forgiveness; but it gives you the choice of some options that you can adapt to your unique situation and comfort level.

Conclusion

The ultimate forgiveness is when you realize that there is nothing to forgive, no victims or persecutors, only volunteers; and that all is an illusion, a set-up for our learning and evolution.

In this school of life there are two kinds of people, *Lovers* and *Teachers*. *Lovers* support us like cheerleaders, and *Teachers* challenge us by giving us something to work on. We need both kinds of people, just like the two paddles in a canoe. A beautiful parable by Neale Donald Walsh in his book *The Little Soul and the Sun* suggests that we are all angels who choose to play different roles so that we can get to experience our divine qualities.

Key Insights

1. Forgiveness is a hygienic act of self-care.

2. We need to forgive because we are the ones who are trapped in the prison created by non-forgiveness.

3. Lack of forgiveness is at the core of many physical and emotional ailments.

4. All forgiveness is a gift of love we give to ourselves. The forgiveness process involves willingness to see the situation through the eyes of Spirit.

5. There are many ways to forgive. You do not have to contact the other person in order to forgive.

Questions to Reflect On

1. Is there anyone in your life whom you need to forgive?

2. Do you have any incomplete issues with anyone?

3. Do you forgive and accept yourself?

Awakening Practice (Forgiveness Meditation)

Take a comfortable posture after doing the necessary preparation, such as going to the washroom and turning off the phone. Now close your eyes and breathe mindfully for a few minutes to settle the mind. Silently say this: "Breathing in, I am aware of the in breath" upon inhalation, and "Breathing out, I am aware of the out breath" upon exhalation. Repeating the phrase helps to promote concentration.

Once the mind is calm, imagine a theatre stage in front of you. You are sitting in the audience and about to watch a forgiveness show. You are the actors, producer, director, and audience of this show. In the first act of this show, you are with somebody you have chosen to forgive. In this scene, you simply express all your feelings to the other person, and his or her role is to simply listen. In the second act, the other person sincerely apologizes to you. In the final act, there is a campfire and a sacred ritual to set you both free. You can create your own ritual, one that especially appeals to you. You and the other person could exchange flowers, gifts, or a hug. You could even imagine angels and light beings showering you both with flowers.

10

CONSCIOUS HEALING

Health is a state of complete harmony of the body,
mind and spirit. When one is free from physical
disabilities and mental distractions, the gates
of the soul open.

B.K.S. Iyengar

It would be ideal to have a healthy body and mind to evolve to our full potential and be the ushers of Heaven consciousness. We typically take our health for granted and only value it after it is lost; therefore, I feel it is very relevant to have a discussion on dealing with illness that sooner or later shows up despite our best intentions to stay healthy.

For over thirty-five years, I have had the privilege of serving as a physician to thousands of clients of all age groups, ethnicities, and racial and religious backgrounds. I try to treat the person rather than the disease; therefore, my approach is different with each person, depending on his/her life experiences, physical and psychological makeup, values, beliefs, motivation, expectations, and treatment preferences.

I have been used as an instrument to treat many, cure some, and comfort and heal most, depending on the degree of receptivity of the person to the holistic approach. My clients continue to be my greatest teachers and have taught me many valuable lessons on the healing effects of love, forgiveness, and faith, and how our healing is intertwined. We seem to have separate minds and bodies but in reality, they are parts of the whole. I have worked through many of my own human challenges in the process of assisting my clients with their issues. Being a physician does not make one immune to the illness and suffering that is inherent in the human condition.

Apart from keeping up with my ongoing professional development, I am also a student and practitioner of yoga, Tai Chi, Chi

Kung, reiki, meditation, mindfulness, and journey work, just to name a few. My therapeutic approach is eclectic, having integrated various psychotherapeutic approaches such as the Satir model, Gestalt, cognitive behaviour therapy, and hypnosis. For the past two years, I have been involved in the study of a consciousness-based medicine, Ayurveda, at the Chopra centre. All this exposure to various modalities has contributed to my holistic approach.

Health and Disease

The Western allopathic model of health is based on the absence of disease. The body is often seen as a biomechanical instrument that behaves like a car. With time, it gets sick and old, has creaky joints, and finally falls apart. For a long time, the mind has been equated with the brain. There is no place in this model for understanding the life force. The focus is on diagnosing and treating disease rather than on the study of health and wellness. All our medications are double-edged swords: while they may ameliorate the symptoms, they can cause troublesome side effects that sometimes are worse than the original condition. The Western model is useful in dealing with acute medical and surgical conditions but falls short in the treatment of chronic conditions.

The holistic model, on the other hand, would view disease as the absence of vibrant health. Our body, mind, and spirit are seen as a living matrix of consciousness, like a flowing river. The Greek philosopher Heraclitus declared, *"You cannot step into the same river twice, for fresh waters are ever flowing in."*

The same is true of the body. Even a single thought can change the whole field. Mind is a process that is in every cell of the body and extends beyond its boundaries. Disease is often seen as a result of imbalance, a call for attention and separation; health is a state of peace and wholeness. The focus is on finding the underlying cause of the disease. Holistic medicine is a system of health care that promotes a co-operative relationship among all those involved, leading toward optimal attainment of physical, psychological, social, and spiritual health.

It emphasizes the need to look at the human being as a living matrix while exploring the physical, nutritional, environmental, emotional, social, spiritual, and lifestyle choices. It incorporates all stated modalities of diagnosis and treatment, including drugs and surgery if no safe alternative exists. Holistic medicine focuses on education and responsibility for personal efforts to achieve balance and well-being.

I use all evidence-based modalities and find both models useful.

Treating, Curing, and Healing

Treating involves amelioration of symptoms of the condition even though the underlying disease process may continue to exist (e.g., diabetes and hypertension).

Curing includes not only the elimination of the cause of the illness but also the tendency toward developing it.

Healing involves facing the illness, owning it, and coming to a place of acceptance and wholeness. For example, an alcoholic might need to face the facts and accept that he has a chronic condition that would require him to abstain from alcohol, keep attending AA meetings, and cultivate an ever-deepening connection with the Higher Power. Healing is to realize that you have a disease but it is not "who you are." In your essence, you are always whole and complete. Healing is about living in the moment fully and accepting all that it offers, both the positive and the negative, with equanimity and grace. Healing is possible even when there is no treatment or cure available. "Healing," "holy," and "wholeness" are all derived from the same word.

Why Do We Get Sick?

There are numerous ailments that can affect the human body, ranging from the common cold to cancer. The earliest physicians thought perhaps illness was a sign of God's anger or the work of evil spirits.

Hippocrates and Galen advanced a theory of *humourism*. According to this theory, we get sick when there is an imbalance of bodily humours (body fluids such as blood, phlegm, black bile, and yellow bile).

Paracelsus was one of the first physicians to suggest that maybe illnesses come from outside sources.

With the advancement of science and medicine, we know that illnesses can be due to a wide variety of factors such as genetics, infectious pathogens (bacteria, viruses, fungi, and parasites), lifestyle choices, poor diet, lack of exercise, stress, psychological trauma, environmental toxins, radiation, coping styles, and so on.

It has been observed that people who cope with their stressful feelings by suppressing them are often vulnerable to develop depression and anxiety, while those who cope by having an angry response are prone to develop hypertension and stroke. People who cope with their feelings by having a rational and logical response are more prone to skin conditions. Finally, people who cope by avoidance or distraction are vulnerable to attention disorders and psychosis. A *congruent person* (chapter seven) is in touch with his/her emotions, that of the other person, and the context. Optimal health is often associated with emotional congruence.[18]

Our body is very dynamic, and even though virtually all of the cells are replaced yearly, yet the disease process still continues. This is because the cell memories of the disease are passed on from the old cells into the new ones. Unresolved guilt feelings are often a subconscious invitation to disease. To fully understand the development and prolongation of the illness, we need to look at all factors, including negative patterns in consciousness that may be contributing to the disease process.

Karmic Theory of Illness

In many spiritual circles, people often talk about karmic reasons for developing an illness. Karma is an Eastern concept. By definition, any thought, word, or deed is karma. Therefore, whatever you sow so shall you reap. It is like a boomerang. All karmas can have a positive, negative, or neutral effect. Further, karma theory rests on the foundation of reincarnation. The lifetime work of Dr. Ian Stevenson on reincarnation and Dr. Brian Weiss's book *Many Lives, Many Masters* present very convincing evidence to the skeptic within us. Our illnesses may be linked with karma from this life or previous lives. People sometimes find karmic theory fatalistic. My feeling is that once you understand it, it can be very liberating.

There are three types of karma:

1. Stored karma or seed karma that has not yet come to fruition (*sanchita karma*)

---

18 See Virginia Satir et al., *The Satir Model* (Palo Alto, CA: Science and Behavior Books, 1991).

2. Unfolding karma from the past that has already come to fruition (*prarabdha karma*)

3. New karma that you are creating in the present moment (*agamic karma*)

Think of an archer who has three kinds of arrows.

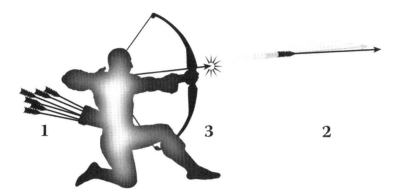

The arrows in his quiver are the stored karma, whereas the arrow in flight is the unfolding karma that has come into fruition. The arrow in his hand is the new karma, with which the archer can change the trajectory of the arrow in flight. Therefore, the point of power is always in the present moment. One can undo lifetimes of negative karma by the choices made now. The following real-life example illustrates this further.

In 1989, I spent a whole month at a yoga ashram doing the yoga teacher training program. Our teacher shared with us a true story of a man who had committed murder in a fit of rage. He was convicted and sentenced. While he was in prison, somebody handed him a book on yoga. He started to practice yoga and meditation and soon became a model prisoner. The prison authorities even accepted his request to attend the yoga teacher training program at the same ashram. Eventually, he was released on parole. He now has his own yoga studio and is a role model for a spiritual lifestyle.

There are many examples of enlightened masters who become ill. Why is that? This may be an act of compassion, as they are working out the karma of their disciples. It may also be one of the infinite mysteries of life. Meditation can also free us by frying the seeds of stored karma to prevent their germination.

What Is Quantum Healing?

The advancement in quantum physics has offered us a new window into the world of form. Everything in the physical domain is a field of vibration.

According to Dr. Deepak Chopra's book, *Perfect Health*, a quantum is defined as the basic unit of matter and, is 10,000,000 to 100,000,000 times smaller than the smallest atom. At this level, matter and energy are interchangeable. Ayurveda (the science of life) claims that the human body starts out as intense but invisible vibrations called quantum fluctuations, before it proceeds to take physical form.

Therefore, if you can influence the quantum field through meditative practice, you can bring about spontaneous and instantaneous changes in the body. The following personal anecdote may illustrate the usefulness of this insight.

> In August 2010, I was scheduled to attend the Perfect Health retreat at the Chopra centre in Carlsbad, California. A few days before the retreat, I came down with severe cold symptoms. Ordinarily, it would take a week to resolve this, with lots of rest, fluids, and maybe some symptomatic treatment. So I seriously thought of cancelling my participation in the retreat. A part of the homework requirement to attend this retreat was to read *Perfect Health*. I decided to apply what I had been learning, so I sat down to meditate. Deep in silence, this prayerful thought of health was released. No medications were taken. The next morning, I got up symptom-free. It seemed like a miracle. I did get to attend the retreat after all.

Practical Suggestions for Healing

- When faced with an illness, get appropriate professional help and do not hesitate to get a second opinion. Collaborate in your care, ask questions, and educate yourself so that you are aware of all treatment options. Healing is much more likely when there is synergy between you and the treating professional. A holistic approach looks at the whole person, and the interventions are at the physical, psychological, and spiritual levels.

• See your illness as a teacher. Consider loving, non-judgmental self-reflection. An illness is the body's way of communicating. Look for unconscious guilt or a pattern that may be attracting this experience of illness. Allow your illness to awaken you to higher levels of consciousness.

• Evoke the healing spirit within through prayer and meditation. Several studies have shown the beneficial impact on patients recovering from major surgery when they are prayed for. It is also through prayer and meditation that the quantum level can be accessed where a single thought can change the whole field.

• Forgive yourself and others. Peace of mind often translates into health. Let go of any emotional baggage. The previous chapter on forgiveness has many practical suggestions on how to forgive.

• Nurture the body through self-care. A massage, good music, or time spent in nature can be deeply nurturing to the body and mind. Health is the body's natural state; allow it to unfold.

• Take things lightly. Cultivate a sense of humour. Norman Cousins, the author of *Anatomy of an Illness as Perceived by the Patient*, overcame a serious illness by laughing his way to health. He would spend his days and evenings watching comedy videotapes. I had the privilege of meeting and working with the legendary Patch Adams who inspired the popular Hollywood movie of that name and brought attention to the healing power of humour.

• Cultivate mindfulness in all activities and practise living in the here and now. While pain is inevitable, the suffering that is created by our ego is optional. It is the ego that keeps track of the past and future and often generates unnecessary worry and anxiety and thereby interferes with the natural healing process.

- Create several "healing intervals" in the day. A healing meditation with or without a CD could be a healing interval. Several of my clients who are treatment resistant or are still having residual symptoms start to improve when they include a few such "healing intervals" in their day. Medical Chi Kung CDs and recordings of Louise Hay and Dr. Bernie Siegel are some of the resources that I have found useful in supporting my clients.

- Think outside the box. I have noticed that people who improve from a treatment-resistant condition are quite willing to try alternative and complementary approaches: hypnosis, Ayurveda, yoga, pranayama, traditional Chinese medicine, acupuncture, Tai Chi, Chi Kung, journey work, homeopathy, and naturopathy, just to name a few.

- Healing affirmations are a powerful way to influence the body and mind. Dr. Émile Coué was able to successfully heal many difficult patients by prescribing them a healing autosuggestion along with the standard remedies. (*Day by day, in every way, I am getting better and better.*) Dr. Coué (1857–1926) was a French psychologist, pharmacist, and a pioneer in hypnosis. He understood the marvellous power of autosuggestion. He stated, "Autosuggestion is an instrument that we possess at birth, and in this instrument, or rather in this force, resides a marvellous and incalculable power." Create your own affirmations.

- Create a support structure of family, friends, and like-minded people around you. There are many groups that offer support and education for various conditions. Check your local resource directory. These days, many people are turning to the web for support. The centre for attitudinal healing offers spiritual guidelines for healing. These guidelines are described in the last chapter, "Being an Usher."

- The recovery process is not a straight path; it often has ups and downs. Therefore, patience and faith are virtues worth cultivating. Some counselling and psychotherapy can be invaluable sources of support.

- There are times when nothing seems to be working, and the

condition continues to deteriorate despite all interventions. Acceptance and surrender to the will of God can still create miracles of healing. In the video *Healing Spirit*, produced by the National Film Board of Canada, there is a story of a psychiatrist who suffered from an intractable case of tinnitus (hearing sounds in the ear). Her life had become unbearable. In acute agony, she found herself on her knees in her kitchen praying to the Lord. It seems someone was listening, as she had a deep spiritual experience and her condition disappeared. The following poem highlights the attitude of acceptance and surrender.

A CREED FOR THOSE WHO HAVE SUFFERED

I asked God for strength, that I might achieve.
I was made weak, that I might learn humbly to obey.
I asked for health, that I might do great things.
I was given infirmity that I might do better things.
I asked for riches, that I might be happy.
I was given poverty, that I might be wise.
I asked for power, that I might have the praise of men.
I was given weakness, that I might feel the need of God.
I asked for all things, that I might enjoy life.
I was given life, that I might enjoy all things.
I got nothing I asked for — but everything I had hoped for.
Almost despite myself, my unspoken prayers were answered.
I am, among men, most richly blessed.

— Roy Campanella

Insights on Aging

Our views about aging continue to change. There was a time when being fifty was considered old, now it is considered rather young. I have a few clients in their seventies who are fitter than many twenty-year-olds. I once met a lady who was in her eighties and running her fifteenth marathon in Ottawa. At age eighty-four, her fitness level was that of a young girl in her twenties. Our body is a living matrix that responds to love and self-care. Therefore, it is possible to reverse or slow down the aging process. I have observed that people who are enjoying what they do often stay younger longer. George Burns, who lived to be one hundred, had this to say about age:

> Age to me means nothing. I can't get old; I'm working. I was old when I was twenty-one and out of work. As long as you're working, you stay young. When I'm in front of an audience, all that love and vitality sweeps over me and I forget my age.

The idea is not to go on living forever but rather to live long enough to realize your true nature and reach the full blossoming of consciousness.

Conscious Dying

Most people have some fear of dying even though they may intellectually know the eternal nature of the self. What people really fear is the suffering they may have to endure and/or the fear of the unknown. Conscious dying is a possibility for all of us as we evolve to higher levels of consciousness. I have known some people who knowingly chose to leave their bodies in a meditative state. They had fulfilled all their worldly obligations, said their goodbyes, and now it was time to leave. Many Buddhist monks practise a particular kind of meditation that prepares them to leave the body at will. Perhaps there will come a time when the process of conscious dying will be available to all of us.

Key Insights

1. Health is a state of complete harmony of the body, mind, and spirit.

2. Our body, mind, and spirit are a living matrix of consciousness, like a flowing river.

3. Disease is a result of imbalance—a call for attention and separation.

4. Healing is possible even when there is no treatment or cure available.

5. Healing is much more likely to occur when there is a

collaborative alliance between you and the treating professional.

6. Acceptance and surrender to the will of God can create miracles.

7. Graceful aging is possible if you have meaning and purpose in your life.

Questions to Reflect On

1. What is your definition of health?

2. How do you feel about using the power of the mind to help the body to heal?

3. What is your purpose for living longer and staying younger?

4. If you suffer from an illness, what lessons/blessings have come from this experience?

5. What are your thoughts and feelings about graceful aging and conscious dying?

Autosuggestions for Health

You can write these healing affirmations on a card, memorize them, put them on your bathroom mirror, and repeat them often, especially before going to bed or upon waking up. You can even modify these autosuggestions to suit your particular needs for healing.

- Every day in every way I am getting healthier and healthier.
- I am becoming a picture of health, light, and well-being.
- I am an infinite being of light; radiant health is my natural state.
- I let go of the pattern in my consciousness that is attracting this experience.
- I invoke the healing power of every point of light within me to release all blocks, imbalances, and negative patterns.
- I love my body and take care of it as I would a sacred temple.
- I don't need this illness and I send it away.
- I am a child of the most High. My health, happiness, success, and liberation are assured.

CREATING HEAVEN
IN RELATIONSHIPS

*The acid test of spiritual growth in people
is the quality of their intimate relationships.*
Vyasa

Most human relationships fall somewhere in a continuum between egoic consciousness and Higher Consciousness. Since we are all evolving, the pendulum could swing more often, especially earlier in our awakening journey until we stabilize ourselves at a higher state of consciousness. We are here in the classroom of our earthly life to learn two main lessons. One is that of unconditional love and the other is forgiveness. *A Course in Miracles* would say that forgiveness is the key to happiness, and, when practised, the blockage to the flow of love is removed.

Love is described as the essence of our being. It is also another name for God. Why then do we still feel the lack of love? We search for it unsuccessfully in relationships. Our human relationships are generally an experience of control drama, love-hate, silent treatments, communication breakdowns, manipulation, highs and lows, disempowerment, and can be a source of considerable distress. Why is that? It is perhaps due to a lack of connection with the source of love. The little me or the ego is often the ruling deity of our lives, and we are seeking the Kingdom of Heaven in the outside world, where it is not. We expect our partner to complete us, make us happy and fulfilled. If one relationship fails, the ego is on the search again for the elusive idea of the perfect partner. Our media, movies, and romance novels feed into this illusion.

In the past thirty years of my practice, I have been a witness to the countless sufferings created by the ego. At an individual, family level, and social level it can present as stress, clinical symptoms of physical or mental illness, conflict, violence, relationship

CREATING HEAVEN IN RELATIONSHIPS

breakdown, instability, and chaos. The same consciousness at the national and international levels has been the cause of our economic problems, poverty, conflict between nations, wars, and terrorism. It is no wonder that the ego has been referred to as *"Maha shatru"* — the "great enemy." I have also watched the miraculous transformation of conflicted relationships into peaceful ones, if one or both partners are willing to awaken and see the other with the loving eyes of the spirit.

Often an awakened person is a straightforward, congruent, kind, loving, giving person with no erroneous zones or control drama. There is a consistency in what they think, say, and do. Through their presence, they have successfully dissolved most, if not all, of their pain body. While on one hand it should be very easy to have a relationship with them, at the same time being around them can be a challenge, since ego wants some reactions, some drama, and gets frustrated when it is not getting the expected feedback.

Scriptures from various wisdom traditions support the thesis that our conflicted human relationships can be transformed into holy relationships if one sees the Divine in oneself and the other person and is willing to totally accept the other person without demanding that he or she change. This is, however, not to be used as a basis to stay in a relationship where there is violence and abuse. One can be unconditionally loving and leave the relationship in peace. The prayer of St. Francis of Assisi, quoted in the final chapter of this book, reflects the great attitude of giving the other person what you really want from him or her — in other words, being the ideal partner yourself rather than seeking one. In the Sikh tradition, the matrimonial ceremony of *Anand Karaj* ("Ceremony of Joy") emphasizes that the relationship is a spiritual practice to see the Divine in creation. This happens by first seeing the Divine in yourself, then in your partner, and eventually in all beings.

Intimate relationships bring to the surface whatever is unresolved. Things may be fine in the beginning of a relationship when both partners are at their best. Once the honeymoon phase is over, the unhealed dysfunctional patterns and pain body start to surface. People are in for a shock when they watch their loving and usually well-mannered partners behaving in an angry and abusive way, as though temporarily possessed. The greatest challenge is to not take your partner's ego and pain personally but to touch it with the gentle hand of loving-kindness and presence. This is a very reward-ing though difficult spiritual practice, but it is this way of being that could dissolve the unhealed past in the present. Alternatively, a reac-tive response perpetuates the karmic cycle of suffering, and the past keeps getting repeated.

An awakened attitude toward the behaviour of others is to rec-ognize that they are either loving or asking for love. When peo-ple are angry or are being vengeful, it is a call for love. But this is only possible if you are in touch with your Higher Self. Socrates was a great example of how he reframed his relationship with his demanding wife, Xanthippe, as a spiritual practice. He was even grateful that she kept him on his toes and helped his spiritual prog-ress. There is a beautiful Sanskrit chant that I often sing as a part of my daily prayers. Its English translation would be: *"May I see the divine in my mother, father, relatives, friends and all relationships."* Our relationships therefore offer us an enriched environment to practise the lessons of love and forgiveness.

It is not necessary for everybody to be in a close, intimate rela-tionship or marriage. Some people can evolve without having to go through the experience of intimate relationship, as long as they are growing and cultivating presence. It is my observation that very few people are suitable for the path of a renunciant, and those rare souls may actually do quite well adopting a monastic lifestyle. The majority of people, though, do need the school of intimate relation-ship to fully evolve emotionally and spiritually. To live the life of a householder and to deal with the challenges of raising a family and manage the practical realities of life can be far more transformative than living in the protected environment of a monastery. I have conversed with people living in various spiritual communities, and many of them are scared of living independently in the world. The distress they experience is similar to that felt by institutionalized patients when discharged into the community. A gradual rehabili-tation is needed before they are ready for independent living. A sign of freedom is when one is adaptable to either environment.

It is important to use all experiences as an opportunity for learning and cultivating presence so that the Heaven consciousness unfolds within us, petal by petal. *The enlightened attitude toward relationships is that they are not here to make us happy but they can help to awaken us.* Since true happiness is an inside job, the outer world can only give us temporary experiences of pleasure and pain — just like a gemologist can tell us if a shiny stone is really a diamond or an imitation. So, too, one needs to have discernment to differentiate between the joy of our true nature and the elusive pleasures of the world. As previously mentioned, the nature of Self is joy, just as the nature of the sun is light and warmth. Therefore, in the school of relationships, we have the opportunity to rediscover who we really are.

The only relationship we are sorting out is our relationship with ourselves. Every outer relationship is simply a reflection of our own relationship with ourselves. The more you are loving and accepting of yourself and are at peace with yourself, the easier it is for you to love and accept everybody else. Whatever you don't accept in yourself, the other person will unconsciously reflect back to you. The most productive attitude is not to blame the mirror but instead to be grateful for being shown an unhealed part of yourself that can now be healed.

As mentioned before, there are only two kinds of relationships, lovers and teachers. Lovers are here to support us in our journey and be our cheerleaders, whereas teachers are mirrors who reflect to us our imperfections and the lessons we need to learn. In intimate relationships, your partner can switch from being a lover to a teacher and back again, many times a day. In the larger sense, we are all each other's teachers and students. We are all wrapped up in our own conditioned patterns like mummies wrapped in bandages. In intimate relationships, we can slowly start to free each other through loving communication, forgiveness of self and the other, learning from our mistakes, and growing in presence.

Empathic listening can be a transformative process. It is the ability to be internally silent and truly listen to the other person from his or her point of reference. The word *LISTEN* has within it all the letters for the word *SILENT*. It is easier to listen and connect with the other person when the Higher Self is in the driving seat. Ego creates walls and internal noise, making it difficult for us to connect in a meaningful way. Relationships offer us an opportunity for practising the *sadhana* (spiritual practice) of staying centred while holding a sacred space for the other.

How to transform
your ego-based relationships
into enlightened relationships

- Start by loving yourself unconditionally and then extending that love to others. This is a complete spiritual practice. Affirmations can be helpful in the initial stages of evolution. Examples of affirmations: *I love and accept myself and others unconditionally. I am capable, lovable, and beautiful exactly as I am.* Affirmations are effective if repeated mindfully.

- Practise listening empathetically; that is, listening from the other person's point of view. It is the ability to walk a mile in your brother's shoes. The more you are able to listen empathetically, the more loving you will be to the people around you, and it often translates into peace, harmony, and healing. Seek to understand first rather than be understood. Be conscious of your body and breath when listening. This would promote inner silence and bring you to the here and now.

- Continue with your daily spiritual practice (*sadhana*). There is no short cut to this. It is your own relationship with yourself that gets reflected in all of your worldly relationships. Like a pro golfer, we, too, need to patiently evolve with regular practice.

- See the relationship as an opportunity for learning and awakening rather than for meeting your expectations. It is human to have expectations, but make them known and be willing to negotiate. In the final analysis, the deep experience of "*the peace that passeth all understanding*" does not happen as long as there are unmet expectations. Expectations are in the domain of ego-seeking fulfillment from the external world. See the difference between expectations, which have an addictive tone, versus preferences, which are much more flexible and liberating. Go deeper than the layer of expectations to the universal yearnings of peace, love, and joy. *The world does not need to change in order for you to feel peace, love, and joy.*

134

- It is not necessary for you to take your partner's pain. You can help dissolve it by being present and not taking it personally. Practise communicating your feelings and needs with loving kindness.

- You can certainly negotiate change, but once again, it is important how the request is expressed. It helps to acknowledge the positive in the other person and then request some changes in a constructive way without its coming across as a demand or an expectation. Practise being a love-finder instead of a fault-finder.

- Keep your perception glasses clean through regular forgiveness of self and others. Remember, this is the only assignment on our earthly school of life. Forgiveness unblocks the inner fountain of love and joy.

- See the relationship as a bank account. Kindness and courtesy are "deposits," while rudeness and insensitivity are "withdrawals." Find out what is a deposit for your partner. You might assume a gift is a deposit; but for the other person, listening or spending time together might be a better deposit than material gifts. With friends, it is easier to keep the account in a positive balance; it is more like a long-term deposit. But in an intimate relationship, the account is a current one, and the balance may change from positive to negative in the same day. So don't take your partner for granted.

- Families or individuals that pray together find a certain connectedness that comes from an experience of shared being. Even if your partner is not interested in praying with you, you can always pray for your partner in silence. However, do not let it become a "holier-than-thou" attitude of the ego. In intimate relationships, spending quiet time with your partner or meditating together can be a great way to feel the love, since love is not in the domain of language; instead, it is a vibration most palpable in silence.

- Life is a like a jigsaw puzzle. You need to always keep the final picture in front of you as you are putting together the puzzle. Similarly, it is crucial to have the final outcome vision of your life in perspective by taking the time to create a personal, couple, and family vision and mission statements. More about this later.

- The tradition of a family meal together can be a very helpful way to keep the circle of family intact, and lines of communication open. Having a weekly family meeting is another opportunity to practise empathic listening and cultivate presence.

- Intimacy needs to be balanced with privacy. There needs to be room in intimate relationships for couple activities as well as individual time. For couples, it is very rewarding to have a weekly "couple date" but not to be rigid about it — allow room for flexibility and spontaneity.

- Written communication can often break the wall of silence when verbal communication has failed. Writing slows down the thinking process, allowing the person to be in touch with his or her deeper thoughts and feelings and to communicate in a constructive and palatable language. The person reading the letter is not triggered and is therefore more likely to get the message.

It would be virtually impossible to find a partner who does not have a pain body. It is advised to use head and heart both when choosing a partner. It is ideal to choose a partner who does not have a heavy pain body. When you marry somebody, you are marrying their pain body as well.

Sometimes it happens that the members of a couple grow at different paces. This may create discord, and if they are unable to resolve the issues, separation may be the logical outcome. Then it is advised that they separate in a peaceful manner and take time to reflect on the lessons learnt before jumping into another relationship quickly. I encourage my clients to work out their differences whenever possible.

Key Insights

1. Forgiveness and unconditional love are the two main lessons in the classroom of life.

2. The enlightened attitude toward relationship is that the other

person is not here to make us happy but they can act as a catalyst for awakening.

3. The only relationship that we are always sorting out is our relationship with ourselves.

4. Listening empathetically is only possible when there is internal silence.

5. The world does not need to change in order for you to feel peace, love, and joy.

Questions to Reflect On

1. What is the quality of your intimate relationship with your near and dear ones? How do you feel as you reflect upon it?

2. How do you deal with unmet expectations in your relationships? Do you habitually keep your feelings to yourself, blame someone, rationalize, or distract yourself?

3. What is your vision of an ideal intimate relationship? How do you feel as you get in touch with this vision?

Awakening Practice
(Self-acceptance Meditation)

Take a comfortable posture and gently close your eyes as you turn within. Now mindfully repeat the following affirmation a few times: *I love and accept myself unconditionally.* Pay attention to your body and mind. Notice if there is any resistance showing up in the form of doubt, disbelief, or tension in the body. Breathe some love and acceptance into the resistance. As you feel calmer, repeat the affirmation again a few times and repeat the process of softening the resistance through love and acceptance. Keep repeating this process until you feel some receptivity within you as you say these words: *I love and accept myself unconditionally.* As you make progress in this practice, you can expand the scope of this affirmation to include others in it. *I love and accept myself and others unconditionally.* Repeat this practice often for a few minutes at a time and watch the miracle of transformation in your relationship with yourself and others.

EFFORTLESS MANIFESTATION

And all things, whatsoever ye shall ask in prayer,
believing, ye shall receive.
Matthew 21:22

A few years ago, my wife and I were at a dinner party in my hometown, Amritsar. The host, a physician, had been a long-term friend and classmate. His wife, a principal of a local coeducational school, had been very influenced by our sharing on spirituality during our previous visits, especially how water crystals can be shaped by our thoughts. Being open-minded, she took the idea of water crystals and had her school children do some research and published an article in their school magazine, which she wanted to present to us. This time, she was eager for us to visit her school the next morning and talk to the children. Without much hesitation, we both said yes and also decided on the spot that the subject would be, "How to make dreams come true."

I can still recall the bright, innocent, and receptive faces of young boys and girls with dreams and ambitions, hanging on to every word that was expressed. During the presentation, I shared with them a personal transformative experience that had shaped my destiny and taught me valuable lessons on how to effortlessly manifest dreams.

> This transformative experience took place in the extremely hot summer afternoon of the year 1971, in the same town. I was sixteen going on seventeen, eagerly waiting to clear my pre-med with high enough marks so that I could apply for entrance into medical school. That afternoon, I was sitting in for my elder brother at his Indian oil dealership shop because he had to step out to deal with some banking matter. I was reading a book

by Napoleon Hill, *The Master-Key to Riches*. The author was stressing the importance of having a dominant purpose and a clear vision. The exercise in the book was to write down your vision of life on a sheet of paper. I took out a letterhead from my brother's stationery supplies and innocently wrote my life vision. I imagined becoming a physician, travelling abroad, learning and teaching. I also created a vision of an ideal personal life and financial prosperity. By the time my brother came back, I had finished the exercise. I folded the sheet of paper and put it in the book and was pleased to be relieved of my afternoon duty so that I could go home and take a siesta in the coolest room on the main floor, unaffected by the sun's scorching heat.

After that incident, I totally forgot about this exercise until seventeen years later, when I agreed to give a sermon at a Unity church in Ottawa on the subject of "Rubbing shoulders with riches and prosperity." While preparing for the service, I decided to consult Napoleon Hill's book, which I had brought to Canada with me. As I opened the book, a paper fell out. I picked it up and curiously read it. To my astonishment, all aspects of my vision had come true.

This, to me, is an example of effortless manifestation. This is a very different way of achieving our dreams, compared to the popular notion that one has to be tenacious and goal-driven like a pit bull terrier to make things happen. Another illustration is that of three ways to get ice cream. The first way is to go and get it yourself. The second way is to delegate and ask somebody to get it for you. The third way is to think about ice cream and allow someone to ask you if you want ice cream. This is obviously the way of effortless manifestation.

While travelling through India, I noticed that the coolies at the train station could always accurately guess, while waiting for the train to arrive, where my executive class coach would end up on the platform.

Effortless manifestation is knowing where to stand on the platform of your consciousness so that the coach of your dreams can stop right in front of you every time.

Another metaphor is that of a light switch. You don't have to be an electrical engineer to turn on the light. Even a child can turn on the light.

Effortless manifestation is knowing where the light switch is.

It is arriving in style at your destination rather than striving. It is the path of the Higher Self vs. ego-based manifestation, which is more like the pit bull approach. One of my favourite inspirational parables is from *Jonathan Livingston Seagull*, by Richard Bach. In this incident, Jonathan's teacher is teaching him how to fly at the speed of thought. He says, "To fly as fast as thought to anywhere that is, you must begin by knowing that you have already arrived." Effortless manifestation is the way to usher Heaven into our lives and on the planet.

Even as I type this chapter on my laptop on April 12, 2006, I am experiencing an effortless manifestation in progress. I am sitting in the breathtaking surroundings of a resort in Kauai, overlooking a golf course, mountains, and waterfalls. I had been praying for the time and space to finish the initial editing of this book. The past few months have been hectic and eventful.

In the month of January, we travelled through India with a cherished couple. It was truly a fulfilling trip, though I did not even get to look at the draft notes of the book. The month of February was equally chaotic, with three deaths in one week: my mother, a nephew, and a very dear friend. So the month of February was busy with late-night phone calls to India, accepting the losses, preparing for the memorial services of three very special souls, and dealing with the demands of an active personal and professional life.

In the first week of March, I was struck by labyrinthitis, an unusual inner ear condition, and ended up in the hospital ER in an ambulance. For a few days, I could barely walk because of vertigo. So when March break arrived, I was not sure if I would be able to handle the stress of travel to Hawaii. I was seriously considering cancelling the trip and staying in Ottawa to catch up with all the things that had been neglected or postponed because of the chaos of the previous two hectic months. Furthermore, I was still not able to drive, due to dizziness.

I did what I preach to my clients. I practised a type of contemplation that involves logical thinking on paper followed by an intuitive process of going within and asking guidance from my inner pilot. The answer came: "Take a leap of faith and go." I saw myself in Kauai watching spectacular sunsets at Hanalei Bay. I had resolved not to drive until comfortable and allow my wife chauffeur me around. So the agreement was that she would do the driving in Kauai.

As it turned out, my wife's driving licence had expired, and the car rental therefore could not be in her name. So the car was issued in my name, and since I was not yet ready to drive for more than a couple of miles, it meant no day trips in Kauai this time. Besides, it had been raining twelve times more than usual for this time of the year, so we were forced to stay indoors at the resort.

The end result was the uninterrupted time and space of two weeks to focus on the book! It almost seems as though the whole universe conspired to create this ideal setting for me to finish the initial editing of previously written chapters and maybe add three more chapters!

The miracles continued to unfold. In two weeks, I did manage to complete the editing of previously written chapters, though I had no time to write the next three chapters. I found myself inwardly praying for some help. I knew that once back in Ottawa, I probably would not find the time and space for a while. In the last week of our holiday, my wife came back from her morning walk and hesitatingly told me that the resort staff had offered to extend our stay in the same unit for a throwaway price, since there had been a last-minute cancellation.

My initial reaction was to say no, since I am a responsible physician and had clients to see, and there were all those pending things to take care of in Ottawa. We agreed to contemplate on it together after dinner that evening. The rest is history. Here I am in my third week, typing this chapter with deep gratitude and knowing without doubt that the Universe has been listening and has answered my prayers.

All the challenges during this trip seemed to be blessings in disguise as well. Sitting for several hours in front of my laptop left me with a stiff neck and back. So I urgently had to get a massage at the spa. There was only one opening that day, and I accepted. My massage therapist happened to be a very spiritual lady. We had an instant connection as though we were kindred spirits. The conversation with her while I lay on the massage table was exactly what I needed to clarify the chapter on "Being an Usher."

According to *A Course in Miracles*, it is normal for us to create miracles. Even the Bible says, "Ask and you shall receive; seek and you shall find; knock and the door shall be opened unto you" (Matthew 7:7). In the Sikh faith there is a hymn, *"Jo mange thakur apne te soi soi deve,"* meaning that whatever you ask of the Lord, He gives. The natural question is, why don't we experience this way of manifestation all the time in our affairs?

Obstacles to Effortless Manifestation

Whenever something is not manifesting in my life or in the lives of my clients, it is usually due to one of these obstacles.

Limiting beliefs and misconceptions

Whatever you believe shall come to pass. Many people have rigid self-limiting beliefs that have never been questioned. Even I used to have this silly notion that I would be bothering God if I asked him for everything. Further, I was raised to believe that we should only say prayers of gratitude.

One summer, we were returning from Kripalu ashram in Lennox, Massachusetts. My wife was driving, and I was listening to Sanskrit chants and contemplating on the subject of what is an appropriate prayer. As I reflected on this, it seemed so silly to be concerned about bothering God with my few prayer requests when He looks after millions of chemical reactions in my body every day to keep me alive and does the same for all beings while managing the whole universe.

During that retreat, I was also introduced to the spiritual life of a sixteenth-century Carmelite lay monk, Br. Lawrence, whose only spiritual practice was to talk to God about anything and everything. From that day onward, I have chosen to have total openness with God about all matters that concern my existence. This simple realization has been very liberating and has empowered me in all aspects of my life. People have limiting beliefs about prosperity, deservingness, God, what to ask for, suffering, fate, etc. The list goes on. I often hear people use expressions such as, *I don't deserve . . . maybe it is not my fate . . . maybe God won't forgive me for my sins . . .*

It is not spiritual to be rich . . . I should not ask God for what I really want. All of the above can stop us from asking for what we really want, and therefore we do not turn on the "manifestation switch."

Lack of clarity

People are so busy coping with life that they don't have the time or luxury of introspection and getting in touch with their heart's desires. Often they are dumbstruck when asked, "So, what do you really want?" Studies have shown that less than 5 percent of the people have a clear written mission, vision, and goals. The Lord is like a gentleman who does not impose His will on you — just like the sun, which would only enter your room if the blinds are open. Even the mother does not give milk unless the baby cries. So take the time to shed light on your inner yearnings. All life experiences offer us a contrast that help us to clarify what we really want.

Lack of congruence

Even though people may be asking for what they desire, very often there is lack of congruence in their thinking, feeling, speech, and behaviour. Some of my female clients in their late thirties look-ing for suitable relationships hear the ticking of their biological clock like a gong. There is an underlying sense of desperation that sends a fearful vibration into the universe that is counterproduc-tive to attracting a partner. In the book *Conversations with God*, the author, Neale Donald Walsh, asks God when his life will take off. A paraphrased version of the elaborate answer by God: "When you start to think, feel, and act congruently." In the Hindu scrip-ture *Bhagavad-Gita*, there is a Sanskrit word for it: *arjvam*, mean-ing integrity of *karma* (action), *vacha* (speech), and *mansa* (mental activity that includes thoughts, images, and feelings). It is said that for a man in *arjvam*, even Providence consults him before writing his destiny.

Egoic dominance

Through the conditioned consciousness of the ego, any manifes-tation is difficult. Even when our dreams are shattered, the ego, like a pit bull, is unwilling to accept the aid of the Higher Self. The following poem beautifully describes the Lord's dilemma in dealing with us.

Broken Dreams

As children bring their broken toys
With tears for us to mend,
I brought my broken dreams to God
Because He was my Friend.
But then instead of leaving Him
In peace to work alone,
I hung around and tried to help,
with ways that were my own.
At last I snatched them back and cried,
"How can you be so slow?"
"My child," He said, "what could I do?
You never did let go."

—Author Unknown[19]

Seven Steps of Effortless Manifestation

The manifestation steps are a synthesis of my insights and timeless wisdom. They are in alphabetical order for easy memorization.

1. *Aspire and connect with the Source.*
    It seems like common sense to get on-line when it comes to working with our computer, yet somehow we ignore the first step of connecting with our Higher Self in the Be/Do/Have paradigm. Without this step, your asking may represent the voice of the ego. This leads to lack of fulfillment in our lives despite outer success. Sometimes, a simple, sincere prayer, "Show me the way," may be all that is needed. Remember, all things are possible when we are aligned with the Source.

2. *Be as specific as possible.*
    Be absolutely clear about what you want. The mind is a domain of confusion as it waxes and wanes like the moon. Protect your dreams from its tendencies. If you ordered a car and forgot to mention a steering wheel, the universe may provide you one without a steering wheel. Writing it down

---

19 I have read this poem in different places. Everywhere it is listed as "Author Unknown" except one entry where there is the name of Robert J. Burdette. Another person, Lauretta P. Burns, claims to be the author of this poem under a different name, "Let Go and Let God."

does help. Thinking on paper is observed to be a common habit of highly successful people.

3. *Create an inner thrill.*
We are all blessed with the faculty of imagination. See the end in mind. Create a sensory-rich imagery and don't just watch it as an observer; step into it as the star of your own movie production. The Olympians who win medals have already seen and felt their success in their imagination long before it happens. Using a vision board, cutting pictures from magazines, or making a PowerPoint presentation of your dream are some of the ways of creating excitement. Take your desire into a silent state of mind and release it like a pebble in still water. This is an act of surrender so that the universe can work its magic in mysterious ways.

4. *Deal with obstacles by repeating the first three steps*
All worthwhile endeavours encounter some obstacles or setbacks. Most people give up their vision or start to question it. This is the time when our commitment is being tested; therefore, go back to the basics and repeat steps 1 to 3 until the manifestation process unfolds in a natural, organic, downstream way.

5. *Expect miracles*
When the above steps are done faithfully, miracles in the form of intuitions, ideas, coincidences, guidance, and synchronicities begin to occur. The right person or a relevant book may show up in your life. Be aware of these miracles and receive them with gratitude.

6. *Follow through*
Follow through these ideas with action. Be relaxed and let go of any concern around the result. Let the universe work out the details. This is karma yoga — action without attachment to the fruit of the action. Letting go of the attachment to the fruits of our effort not only hastens the process of manifestation, it also improves the quality of the action itself.

7. *Experience gratitude consciousness*
This is usually the internal state of people who are virtuosos in effortless manifestation. Gratitude is the key that opens God's treasury. Accept all outcomes as blessings and opportunities

for learning. Gratitude is also the antidote to the ego so that Master Supreme can work His magic.

*The most power*ful prayer is to be thankful for all that we have received and all that we have not.

The magic really happens when attachment is released.

Affirmations for Building Faith

Over the years, I have found these affirmations very supportive in building the muscle of faith. Affirmation when properly done evokes the universal power of the spoken word (*Matrika Shakti*).

I have faith even when there is outer uncertainty.

I know that God is the ultimate source of all my good.

I have faith that God will find ways. With God all things are possible.

I believe that the Lord gives what I ask for, and I am eternally grateful.

I am co-creator of my destiny and all my experiences.

I am grateful for all that I have received and all that I have not.

Virtuosos in the Art of Effortless Manifestation

I would also like to express gratitude to all my teachers who modelled for me the art of effortless manifestation. One such person was Sri Chinmoy. His life and works provide an example of a master in the art of effortless manifestation.

Key Insights

1. Effortless manifestation is to know where to stand on the platform of your consciousness so that the coach of your dreams can stop right in front of you every time.

2. Our egoic consciousness with its limiting beliefs, lack of congruence, and lack of clarity gets in the way of effortless manifestation.

3. "Ask and it will be given unto you" is a universal teaching in most sacred traditions.

4. Gratitude is the key to God's treasury. Being grateful for what you have creates a vibration that allows more good to come your way.

5. Be very clear about what you desire; create an inner thrill and let the universe work out the details.

Questions to Reflect On

1. How do you generally manifest your desires?

2. What do you really want to create in your life?

3. What is getting in the way of your dreams?

Awakening Practice
(Meditation for Manifestation)

Think of something you want to manifest and the reasons for manifesting it. Ask yourself if it is in alignment with your highest good. Now create a preview of it in your mind. You are the producer and director of your mental movie. Make it alive and walk into it. Ask yourself, what if it came true? Wouldn't that be wonderful? Surround this vision with a pink bubble and release it to the universe as you silently say this prayer, "Let this — or whatever is better for me — happen."

13

PERPETUAL JOY IS POSSIBLE

Since joy is the goal of all goals, therefore nothing less than perpetual joy would satisfy us.

Vyasa

It was March 19, 2001, and we were spending spring holidays on the lush island of Kauai. I had not slept well for a few nights, perhaps due to the time difference, getting used to new surroundings, and the all-night calls of roosters. Here I am in paradise, yet my body and mind are not happy. My morning routine usually is to have a cup of tea and read the *Daily Word* and then do some meditation or yoga, or take a walk, depending upon inner guidance. So I opened the lesson on *Daily Meditations: Practicing the Course* by Karen Casey. The lesson happened to be, *"Perpetual Joy Is Possible."* My initial impulse was to take the book and throw it across the room. The idea of perpetual joy seemed so dissonant to my feelings of frustration, disappointment, and exhaustion at that moment!

Despite a great deal of inner resistance, I decided to read the daily lesson anyway. The key points in the reading were as follows:

- *Nothing really matters, and this experience is merely an illusion.*

- *Regardless of how a situation looks, it holds no command over us.*

- *All experiences are simply learning opportunities.*

- *We are completely in the care of God through the presence of the Holy Spirit in each moment.*

- *Joy is our prerogative, and we do have the ability to choose.*

The message felt like somebody had applied salt to an open wound. After the meditation, I decided to reread the lesson. It felt somewhat softer. I decided to go on a gentle, mindful walk to contemplate on the message while enjoying the lush, green landscape of Princeville, Kauai. I do not know when the shift happened, but suddenly, as though a cloud had been lifted, my mind and body were in the moment and my mood was that of acceptance, lightness, and joy. This joyful consciousness stayed with me through rest of the holidays. It was indeed a miracle!

We returned to Ottawa at the end of March. Our children came to receive us at the airport. My daughter informed me there had been a phone call from India about my father's health. As soon as I arrived home, I called India and found out my father had had a stroke and was in a coma. I did not know whether to take the next plane to India or stay on the phone and provide support to my mother by being available instead of being en route for a couple of days. After a few prayerful moments, I decided to stay in Ottawa and spent the next two weeks on the phone consulting with the physicians who were looking after my father, providing moral support to my mother, and praying for the highest will in this situation. Because of about a twelve-hour time difference, most of my phone calls were quite late at night.

One night, I went to bed in a very prayerful mood, after having a long chat with my mother; there had been no improvement in my father's condition. I lay in bed, gently folded my hands over my chest, and soulfully started to pray for Divine Will for my father and sending him loving kindness blessings. I noticed my awareness floating up and down a hollow, dimly lit shaft. Suddenly, I broke through the shaft and found myself facing many suns of brilliant white light and a panoramic view of space and planets. I am not sure how long I stayed in that state but then I suddenly snapped back into body awareness with an unearthly feeling of joy, and every cell of my body was pulsing with aliveness. With the feeling of joy came acceptance and peace to face whatever scenario Divine Will might create. My father passed away peacefully on Easter day, leaving me with a deep sense of gratitude at this miracle.

This is one of many experiences I have been blessed with where it has become clear to me that perpetual joy is possible if we practise looking at the world with the eyes of Spirit rather than the limited perspective of our conditioned mind.

What Is Joy?
And How Is It Different
from Pleasure and Happiness?

After some contemplation, I have come to see a continuum where pleasure/pain and negative emotions are on one end, peace, love, and joy are on the other end, and contentment, acceptance, and happiness are in the middle. One metaphor is that of alcoholic drinks like beer, wine, cognacs, hard liquor, etc. They all contain alcohol in different percentages. Pure joy would be akin to 100 percent alcohol. It is no wonder that many saintly people have referred to this state of bliss and joy as an intoxicating experience. The joy scale may look like this:

Enlightened state of unity consciousness

Joy/love/gratitude/peace

Passion/ enthusiasm/happiness

Contentment/hopefulness/optimism

Acceptance

Neutrality and detachment

Boredom/pessimism

Pleasure/pain and frustration

Negative emotional spectrum:

Disappointment, worry, blame, anger, jealousy, guilt, fear, and despair

The world of names and forms can give us only transitory experiences of pleasure and pain, which we often confuse with the real, lasting experience of happiness and joy that is not dependent on anything external. For example, eating good food can be pleasurable to a degree, but if you go beyond moderation, you may suffer the discomfort of overeating and indigestion. The same is true for sex, alcohol, material objects, and relationships. All worldly accomplishments, name and fame can be a great ego boost initially, but once the high is over, there is again the void and anticlimax, and the search for another challenge to feel good again.

A surgeon friend of mine is very successful from a worldly perspective, yet whenever I meet him, he is often frustrated because he wants to take his success to the next level; the current status is never good enough for him. In a way, we are all no different from him, since it is so easy to get enchanted with the world of form — that is why in the East it is referred to as *maya* (illusion). It is *maya* that makes us pursue the ever-elusive mirage in the desert of forms while the oasis that we seek is within.

The peace and joy that one experiences after a meditation, a quiet retreat, or time spent in nature comes from within and does not have any outer cause or negative side effects associated with it. Like a good gemologist, we need to be shrewd and develop the discrimination to separate out the zircons of momentary pleasures from the diamonds of joy that are found within. As mentioned in the ancient Vedic scriptures, our essential nature is *Sat Chit Ananda* (truth, awareness, and joy).

Why Seek Joy?

The world is a classroom, and pain is one of the ways we grow and learn, although it is not always the case. In my practice, I see many clients who have endured more than their share of pain and suffering, although it has still not motivated them to take a U-turn and look within for answers. The hard shell of the ego is difficult to crack. In India, this is symbolically ritualized by breaking open a coconut before any worship ceremony.

Then there are people who begin to awaken consciously following a tragedy or even a minor setback. It is a sign of Grace when somebody starts to awaken. Once a certain level of awakening is reached, avoiding pain need no longer be the incentive to grow. *We can now grow faster with joy and awareness. Buddha, in his teachings on the seven factors of enlightenment, listed joy as one of the factors.*

What do we really want through all of our accomplishments, relationships, and the material world of form? Ultimately we all yearn for something formless such as happiness, love, peace, joy, fulfillment, passion, etc. *In the final analysis, joy and happiness are the goal of all goals.* Since the nature of Self is joy, it is always one with the Divine. Therefore, what we are actually seeking is the Divine, and we don't even know it. The mystic poet Rumi said it so poignantly:

Friend, you seek the formless,
You are actually seeking the beloved
And don't even know.

Happiness Research

The state of happiness and joy is very nourishing and healing for the body and mind. It is nature's best antidepressant. It simultaneously releases opiates, dopamine, oxytocin, and serotonin. These are also immunomodulators and protect us from infections, cancer, and autoimmune diseases. King Solomon said it eloquently: *"A merry heart doeth good like a medicine."*[20]

Research on happiness would tell us that happiness is affected by our early childhood conditioning, conditions of living, and voluntary actions that we take to seek it. The take-home point from all of that voluminous research is that no matter how bleak and gloomy our situation may look, we can still experience happiness and even change our conditioning. Fortunately, we are living in a time where there are lots of therapeutic options available for people who are suffering from not just existential unhappiness but clinical depression. *In the final analysis, happiness is a choice.*

How to Enhance Your Joy Quotient

Once the "why" to pursue joy is clear, the "how to" becomes easier to discover. I have offered you a buffet of practical suggestions arranged in alphabetical order. Each of these suggestions is like a ray of sunshine: when pursued, it can invariably lead you back to the source of all joy.

A to Z of How to Cultivate Joy

• **Aspire** *with every breath.*

Aspiration is an expression of our soul's cry to ascend toward heaven. If you are feeling positive, hopeful, enthusiastic, and uplifting emotions, then the aspiration-flame within you is burning brightly. When you are bogged down by life and are feeling very heavy and discouraged, it is a sign that you need to stoke the fire of

---

20   Proverbs 17:22.

aspiration again. Practising moment-by-moment connection with the higher power can be an effective way to keep the aspiration-flames ascending like the peaks of Mount Everest. Joy comes naturally when you are aspiring with every breath.

- *Put* **Being** *before doing.*

We are human beings, not human machines. Therefore, practise pausing often. Take time to smell the flowers. Give your full attention to whatever you are doing and make the present moment your friend. Cultivate mindfulness in all activities and you shall be blessed with a wellspring of joy within you regardless of outer conditions.

- **Choose** *being happy over being right.*

The conditioned mind or the ego within us likes to be right and would usually sacrifice happiness to get the last word. The ego is not our friend. We forget that we are all looking at the same elephant of reality through different windows. Therefore, we are bound to have different points of view. The opposite of right can also be right. The ego has a hard time accommodating a competing narrative, since it sees the world in duality: black and white, right and wrong, good and bad, sinners and saints, etc. Be the first one to say, "Maybe you are right," or, "I am sorry," and watch the magic of healing and joy in your relationships unfold.

- *Perform* **Daily** *self-care and spiritual practice.*

The music of joy can play only on a well-tuned instrument. Daily self-care involves taking care of your body, mind, and spirit like a temple. Just like a concert pianist or a professional golfer, we need to practise the art of perfecting our nature. The helpful attitude is one of love and self-acceptance rather than trying to fix ourselves out of fear or self-criticism. We are all gods in embryo form, and self-care is creating the sacred space for the embryo to evolve.

- **Embrace** *what is.*

A dysfunctional relationship with the present moment is one of the definitions of the ego. The ego is rarely pleased with *what is* or with the present moment. Acceptance of *what is* does not mean resignation; it is an essential step on the way to transformation. Krishnamurti, the great Indian philosopher, once asked his long-term disciples if they wanted to know the secret of his spiritual attainment. Everybody was curious, even though they had been listening to him for years. His simple and yet profound answer was, "I don't mind what happens."

No matter what is happening in your life, try this mantra: "*It is okay. All is in Divine order, even though it may not be clear to me right now.*"

• **Forgive** *yourself and others.*

Being unforgiving toward self and others blocks the fountain of joy within us. Forgiveness is our quintessential assignment on this earthly plane. As long as we are still bound by our conditioned, ego-driven mind, we need to forgive ourselves and others. Once we awaken from the dream of illusion, it becomes obvious that there was nothing to forgive. It was all a set-up for healing.

• *Cultivate* **Gratitude** *consciousness.*

Gratitude is that great attitude that transforms the base metal of suffering into the gold of joy and healing. *One of my spiritual mentors used to say that the fare from earth to heaven is the gratitude-fragrance of your heart.* It is the golden key that unlocks the doors to God's treasury of blessings and grace. It is easy to be thankful when things are going well, but the real test is when adversity appears. Create a memoir of happy and grateful moments and share them with your loved ones and the world.

• *Engage in* **Hobbies** *and passions.*

Seek pleasures that are good for you and contribute to your awakening. If your work is intellectual, find a hobby that takes you out of your head, such as a sport or a craft. A hobby can offer relief from the tormenting mind. We in North America sometimes consume an excessive amount of TV and Internet; therefore, keep a close watch on your media habits. Choose programs that uplift you and promote awakening.

• **Inspire** *yourself with uplifting reading, listening, and viewing.*

We live in "interesting times," and there are so many options for us. Depending on your preference, you can learn in so many different ways. Uplifting thoughts keep stoking the aspiration flame within us. I once had a client who transformed her depressive state by simply reading inspiring stories in the popular *Chicken Soup for the Soul*.

• *Experience the* Joy *of singing, laughter, fun, and play.*

You cannot enter the Kingdom of Heaven unless you have a child-like nature. Can you laugh easily and freely? Laughter is very healing for our body, mind, and spirit. Where there is seriousness, there is ego. Look for the humour in life.

You don't have to be a professional singer in order to experience the joy of singing. Every bird has a song to sing, not just the nightingale. I recently discovered the amazing karaoke machine, which has made us all feel like singers and provided hours of joy and fun. Once you stop judging and comparing your talent, singing can be really enjoyable.

Many years ago, I attended a few retreats with a spiritual group that offered some games for the adults. Initially, most people would be shy; then as they would start playing, the spontaneity within them would emerge. After the games, our meditations were effortless, deep, and blissful. Embrace the child within you. The universe is your playground.

• *Have Karuna — compassion for all beings.*

What you send out comes back like a boomerang. When you see the underlying unity of life, compassion comes naturally. What you give to your brother you give to yourself. There is a beautiful Sanskrit prayer: "*Loka Samastha Sukhinow Bhavantu,*" "May all beings be blessed." Compassion does not mean that you have to take on the world's pain. Even Mother Teresa had to say no sometimes so that she could do some self-care. Compassion is the natural outcome of that consciousness of connectedness. Compassion opens the heart and unblocks the fountain of joy within us.

• Love *yourself and others unconditionally.*

As they say, charity begins at home. In order to love our neighbour, we need to cultivate a loving relationship with ourselves. What we do not accept within ourselves will bother us in another person. The world is a classroom and it mirrors all that is unhealed within us. The next time you look at yourself in the mirror, bring to surface a deep feeling of love and acceptance toward yourself. Notice your joy quotient increase as you practise self-love and acceptance. Some affirmations for this practice are:

I love and accept myself and others unconditionally.
I am capable, lovable, and beautiful exactly as I am.

• *Have Mudita — sympathetic joy at the success of others.*

We are all interconnected and therefore when any one of us succeeds, we all progress. The seeds of jealousy sprout only in the field of separation consciousness. Our left arm is not jealous of our right arm because it is stronger. We are all parts of the same cosmic body and our sense of separation is nothing but an illusion created by our senses and the brain. In the East, they would call this illusion *maya*. Quantum physics also confirms our unity at a vibration level.

• *Seek* **Nirvana** *through non-judgment.*

The most perfect choice in an imperfect world would be that of no judgments of the self and others. By judging anything, we break reality up into fragments; but the universe is not a mosaic of fragments. There is wholeness and unity in God the creator and the creation. Judgment is the domain of the ego. Seen from the eyes of the spirit, even this imperfect world with its outward seeming chaos has an underlying order and beauty. Similarly, look at your own life with the non-judgmental consciousness of acceptance and wonder at the mystery of this existence.

• *Promote an* **Optimistic** *outlook on life.*

Our early childhood experiences have a significant impact on our outlook of the world. You may habitually see the world as a cup that is half full or half empty. But with some conscious effort, you can train yourself to look for silver linings in the clouds. A positive mental attitude can bless your life with enthusiasm, success, and happiness.

• *Find* **Peace** *and equanimity when faced with adversity.*

The real test of your spiritual growth is how you face adversity. We always have a moment-by-moment choice between peace and conflict. Underneath all of our human upsets, there is a substratum of peace. Bring to these situations acceptance and surrender and watch your consciousness shift. Love, peace, and joy are the essential qualities of the Self.

• Question *all spiritual teachings, beliefs, and perceptions.*

It is only through the process of sincere enquiry, contemplation, and meditation that we can awaken to the transcendent nature of joy. If a spiritual teaching does not free us from suffering, it is important to enquire into it like a sincere scientist. We need to have a non-judgmental look at our beliefs, values, and perceptions to ensure they are aligned with the highest wisdom of unity consciousness.

• Rest, Relax, and Renew.

In the modern world, we can neither work with satisfaction nor rest properly. This imbalance between work and rest leads to a buildup of stress in our minds and bodies and makes us vulnerable to illnesses. An active life needs to be balanced with periods of rest, relaxation, and renewal. Nature is like a mother who heals all of our worldly stress with her gentle embrace. Spend some time in nature every week and let her stillness remind you of your own eternal nature and oneness with all life.

• Serve *in whatever ways you are inspired.*

Service is the rent we pay for living on the planet. The attitude of service prepares the heart and mind for transcendental joy. It may be as simple as helping someone to cross the road or a silent prayer. As you awaken, compassion and kindness arise naturally toward all beings. Practise random acts of kindness.

• Transform *addictive desires into preferences.*

Desires move us out of inaction, though not all desires are liberating. Some interpreters of Buddhist teachings may refer to desires as the root cause of all suffering. It is obvious that not all desires are binding; for example, the desire for liberation. It is virtually impossible to create a life without desires. One of my teachers would often say, "It is okay to have desires as long as you are able to manage them." Preferences are more liberating than addictive desires. Actually, things come more naturally when one is not obsessed with the outcome.

• *Develop* **Unity** *consciousness.*

Non-dualistic consciousness is the state of a liberated person. In unity consciousness, there are no thoughts, concepts, or subject-object distinction. Our ordinary consciousness includes sleep, wakefulness, and dreams. During meditation, we access the fourth, or transcendent state. As the meditation deepens, one is able to access higher levels of consciousness, culminating in unity consciousness, where all duality dissolves.

• **Visualize.**

Visualization is the forerunner of realization. We are blessed with this faculty that can allow us to manifest all that we want, including enlightenment, which is a state of perpetual joy, bliss, and connectedness. Cultivate this faculty and be the co-creator of your destiny.

• *Cultivate* **Wisdom,** *the answer to all problems.*

Wisdom is different from book knowledge or information. It is the essence of our experiential knowledge. Wisdom is like the perfume produced by distillation of the essence of a large amount of flowers. Even a small drop of perfume is enough to fill a room with its fragrance. *Wisdom is not intellectual. It is atomic, whereby every atom of the body is imbued with the knowing that can liberate us from this illusion of ignorance and suffering.* So cultivate wisdom through regular spiritual practices of self-study, meditation, enquiry, and contemplation. All joy, love, peace, and kindness have their roots in wisdom.

• *Avoid* **Xtremes.**

In order to play a piece of music, the string instrument has to be perfectly tuned, not too tight or too loose. Similarly, a life of balance and moderation is in alignment with the highest vibration of pure consciousness of *sattva.* Unless one is vigilant, modern life with all its varied temptations can easily lead to an imbalance. Many people find it hard to go to bed at a decent time because of the temptations of TV, the Internet, and other distractions that are the gifts of modern times. We need to consume food in measured doses, yet most of us have a hard time resisting the temptations of foods that are tasty but not good for us. In order to experience a life of joy and peace, moderation and balance are essential disciplines. The good news is, as we grow in awareness, it becomes easier to say no to temptations.

- **Yearn** *for transcendental joy and liberation.*

The Sanskrit word for this yearning is *"Mumuksha."* Only a few souls are ready for awakening at a young age. Most people need to go through a period of ignorance and fascination with the world of form. It is only through disenchantment, suffering, illness, or a tragedy that we may start to look within for liberation from this world of form. Suffering does not necessarily lead to awakening. In the final analysis, it is by divine grace that this journey begins.

- *Connect with the* **Zero-point field.**

When there is no separation between the subject, object, and the process of observation that is the state of unity consciousness, in terms of modern-day quantum physics, you would be in the zero-point field, when you are beyond time and space, everywhere and nowhere now. A Hawaiian psychiatrist apparently closed a psychiatric ward by practising the Ho'oponopono (ho-o-pono-pono) prayer. This is an ancient Hawaiian practice of reconciliation and forgiveness. Similar forgiveness practices were performed on islands throughout the South Pacific. The prayer is as follows:

- I love you
- I am sorry
- Please forgive me
- Thank you

He simply would connect with the consciousness of each person and heal him or her by practising forgiveness and unconditional love.

How to Connect with Joy When Life Is Stressful

It is easy to be joyful when life is going well and there are no challenges. Stress, however, is inevitable, and the real test of our wisdom is how quickly we bounce back from our negative state into joy. Here are some simple suggestions.

- **Accept what is.** Acknowledge your feelings. Give yourself some psychological air. Denial and suppression of feelings never helps. Similarly, wallowing in your feelings reinforces the conditioned self. It is the state of *presence* that allows us to accept our feelings.

- **Surround** your non-peace with peace. Be still, if it is practical in your circumstances. Connect with the aliveness in your body and do not judge.

- **Remember** that this, too, shall pass. Nothing in this world of form is permanent.

- **Evoke radical gratitude** for this challenge. With every crisis, there is a blessing of equivalent or more value.

- **Call upon the Higher Self** for guidance if you are comfortable with praying. Pray, meditate, and journal if possible; or simply ask for help from the wisdom within.

- **Practise being in the here and now.** The ego's conditioned patterns cannot stand the light of this moment.

- **Let go** of any attachment to the outcome. That is the essence of karma yoga.

- **Know that joy is the nature of the Self.** It is like the sun that is always shining even though our emotional sky may feel dark and gloomy at this moment.

Joy and the Law of Attraction

There is confirmation of the Law of Attraction in most traditions. Simply speaking, we are creating our life by what we focus on. Recently, this law was brought into our everyday consciousness by the popular book and documentary movie, *The Secret*. In short, the Law requires of us to ask for what we want and to align with it through *allowing*. If something we need is not coming to us, it could be due to our resistance. A state of joy is a condition of nonresistance. People, opportunities, and circumstances will come to you naturally and synchronistically. It is the universe giving you a red carpet treatment.

Key Insights

1. The world of form and objects can give us only transitory experiences of pleasure and pain, which we often confuse with the lasting joy that comes from within.

2. As we awaken, we realize that we do not need pain and suffering in order to grow. We can actually grow faster with joy and awareness.

3. Joy is very nourishing and healing to the body and mind.

4. We can consciously enhance our joy quotient and be established in perpetual joy.

5. As we awaken, it becomes easier to bounce back to joy from a negative emotional state.

Questions to Reflect On

1. How do you feel right now? (Pay attention to your body; if there is a discrepancy between body and mind, the body is usually right.)

2. What is your emotional response to the message that perpetual joy is possible?

3. When was the last time you felt really relaxed and joyful? Reflect on that experience.

Awakening Practice (Meditation for Joy)

Imagine a glorious sunrise or sunset that you may have seen in the past; or just a fantasy. Let all your senses come alive as though you are experiencing it now. Visualize a flock of birds flying into the sun. Their bodies shine like gold. What if you are one of those birds? How would you feel? If this creates joy and wonder in you, then let your mind roam free and play with this vision for a few minutes. Notice how you feel at the end of the process.

BEING AN USHER

Child of God, you were created to create the good,
the beautiful and the holy.
A Course in Miracles

Who Is an Usher?

Anyone who is consciously awakening is an usher of heaven. It is not about becoming somebody special or doing something to transform the world. It is about being guided by your Higher Self, embracing the world with all its imperfections, and allowing your love and light transform it. As an usher, you move about in the world like a lighthouse and your mere presence removes the negativity of darkness around you.

Being an usher is to know that your healing is intertwined with that of your fellow beings. There is willingness to awaken from the dream of illusion that we are all born into. There is a growing realization that giving and receiving are one, and therefore, all that you give to others is given to yourself. It is about remembering who you really are. Being an usher is to know that you are divine and your true nature is peace, love, and joy. To be an usher is to be willing to allow the spirit to make you an instrument of Divine will. An usher knows that the most precious moment is this moment, and the Kingdom of Heaven is here and now. An usher touches life with presence.

You don't have to be perfect or fully blossomed in your consciousness in order to be an usher. Sincere willingness to see reality differently is all that is required. You are ready to awaken when you find yourself saying that there has to be another way to go through life rather than being mired in the status quo of suffering. As you awaken, the world of illusion becomes a classroom for learning and growth, and all situations and circumstances are viewed as a part of the learning curriculum. *To awaken consciously and leave the world a little better place is to have succeeded as an usher.* While visiting a public garden in New Delhi, India, I saw this verse of Urdu poetry at the entrance. The verse captures the humble intention of an usher. Here is the English translation of it:

"I realize that I could not create a beautiful garden on this ground but at least I managed to clear up some weeds and remove some thorns from the way."

An usher is a *Bodhisattva*, which is the Pali word for one who is awakening to eventually become a *Buddha* (the awakened one).

The word usher inspires trust, a helpful attitude, willingness to serve, gentleness, and patience. It seems that the word "USHER" is a perfect acronym:

Unity An usher is aspiring to be in "unity consciousness" rather than separation consciousness.

Service An usher understands the value of "service" as a spiritual practice, since giving and receiving are one.

Harmony An usher aspires to the higher vibrations of "harmony" and, in the process, promotes healing and happiness for the self and others. The silent prayer of an usher is, *"May all beings be blessed."*

Expansion An usher is consciously "expanding his/her consciousness" through regular spiritual practice.

Reverence An usher has "reverence" toward all life, and sacredness is internalized.

In this concluding chapter, I am reviewing some of the suggestions to assist readers to continue to aspire and awaken to their full potential. Though some ideas may seem repetitious, the intention is simply to be helpful.

1. Create a Personal Transformational Creed.

In 1991, I was inspired to create a personalized transformational creed, which to this day has been illuminating my way like a lighthouse. It was in February 1991. I came home from work, and we were all supposed to be with our music teacher, who had accepted our whole family as his students. But somehow the spirit within had a different agenda. I had been very inspired by the book *The Greatest Salesman in the World* by Og Mandino. Earlier that day, I had even prayed for a creed that would support me in my spiritual life. So I excused myself from the music class and sat on the lounging chair in our bedroom and composed this creed. Even to this day it inspires me. I would like to share it with you in the hope that you will be inspired to create your own creed that would bring out the highest and best in you. Since the creed is several pages long, it has been placed in the Appendix A for easy access.

I am thankful that I listened to the guidance of the spirit, even though I may have annoyed the music teacher and my family members by missing the music class. I did make an audio recording of the creed over a background of Pachelbel's *Canon*. I would listen to it often while driving, exercising, or going for a walk.

2. Live a Mission-directed Life.

Life is like an elaborate, living, jigsaw puzzle with millions of pieces. Unless you have the final picture in front of you at all times, it is impossible to put together even a 500-piece puzzle. In this context, I am using the word "mission" as synonymous with the terms "outcome goal," "purpose," or "vision." This is very different than our usual exercise of goal-setting. In the jungle of life, a clear mission offers us a compass that can help us find our way out of the confusion. I found it extremely valuable to take the time to create a mission/vision statement not only for my life but also for my relationships, family, and the world.

By being visionaries, we co-create reality. Imagine the immense influence of Martin Luther King's historic speech, "I have a dream . . ." The power of visioning is emphasized in most scriptures, including the Bible: "*Where there is no vision, the people perish*" (Proverbs 29:18). Examples of my personal, family, and world vision are in the Appendix A for your perusal. A mission statement is not a static trophy that you put in a showcase. It needs to be kept updated and fresh like a new sunrise each morning. In order for it to be effective, it needs to be dynamic and internalized so that it can guide all our thoughts, choices, and actions.

3. Draw Inspiration from Scriptures.

The wisdom within scriptures can be very transformative if one is receptive, like an oyster who can transform any particulate matter, no matter how small, into a pearl. It is imperative, when reading or listening to scriptures, to try not to get into an intellectual discussion. Just sit with the wisdom in silence and let it water the seeds of awakening within you. Many well-meaning people lose the benefit of a spiritual practice by engaging in a heated debate over the meaning of the scripture. Jesus used "The Parable of the Sower" to stress the significance of having a receptive state of mind.

> A farmer went out to sow his seed. As he was scattering the seed, some fell along the path, and the birds came and ate it up. Some fell on rocky places where it did not have much soil. It sprang up quickly, because the soil was shallow. But when the sun came up, the plants were scorched, and they withered because they had no root. Other seed fell among thorns, which grew up and choked the plants. Still other seed fell on good soil, where it produced a crop — a hundred, sixty or thirty times what was sown. Whoever has ears, let them hear (Matthew 13: 3–9).

Repetition of the scripture is a wonderful way to drive the wisdom deep within the cells and molecules of the body. The late Swami Chinmayananda once while visiting Ottawa gave us the assignment of reading chapter seven of the *Bhagavad-Gita* (a Hindu scripture) a total of eleven times in six months by reading two verses every day and contemplating on them. By the seventh revision, the words had become alive for me, and each verse would bring tears of aspiration.

Since then, I have tried this kind of approach to other books and scriptures with similar results. Some people prefer to read; I find it more practical and even fruitful to listen more often than reading. Sometimes it is hard to discipline yourself to study the scriptures on a regular basis, and at those times, joining a community of like-minded seekers can be very supportive. For me, a scripture is not just a religious book but any book or audiovisual material that can make me aspire to the realms of higher consciousness. In the final analysis, all wisdom that you ever need is within you, and you can access it in stillness; as the biblical saying goes, *"Be still, and know that I am God"* (Psalms 46:10).

For the reader's inspiration, I have included a few of the scriptural passages and quotes that I have come to cherish over the years.

PRAYER OF SAINT FRANCIS OF ASSISI

Lord, make me an instrument of Thy peace.
Where there is hatred, let me sow love;
Where there is injury, pardon;
Where there is doubt, faith;
Where there is despair, hope;
Where there is darkness, light;
Where there is sadness, joy.

O Divine Master, grant that I may not so much to be consoled as to console;
To be understood, as to understand;
To be loved, as to love.

For it is in giving that we receive.
It is in pardoning that we are pardoned,
and it is in dying that we are born to Eternal Life.
Amen.

ANYWAY[21]

If people are unreasonable, illogical, and self-centred,
LOVE THEM ANYWAY

If you do good, and people accuse you of selfish, ulterior motives,
DO GOOD ANYWAY

If you are successful, you could win false friends and true enemies;
SUCCEED ANYWAY

The good you do could be forgotten tomorrow;
DO GOOD ANYWAY

Honesty and frankness will make you vulnerable;
BE HONEST AND FRANK ANYWAY

What you spent years building may be destroyed overnight;
BUILD ANYWAY

21 This poem hangs in Mother Teresa's Sisters of Charity house in India.

People really need help but may attack you if you help them;
HELP PEOPLE ANYWAY

Give the world the best you have and you could get kicked in the teeth;
GIVE THE WORLD THE BEST YOU'VE GOT ANYWAY

— Anonymous

EIGHT STEPS TO HIGHER CONSCIOUSNESS

Step 1: I surrender.

I admit that, of myself, I am powerless to solve my problems; powerless to improve my life. I need help.

Step 2: I believe.

I believe that a power greater than myself—the Holy Spirit—is with me at all times and responds whenever I ask.

Step 3: I understand.

I understand that ego-based false perception makes my problems, failures, unhappiness, and fears appear real. I understand that by asking the Holy Spirit to see differently, my life can be transformed.

Step 4: I decide.

I choose the consciousness of the Holy Spirit, releasing my false perceptions and allowing the Holy Spirit to decide for God for me.

Step 5: I forgive.

I am willing, with the help of the Holy Spirit, to forgive all illusions I have held and all mistakes I have made. I forgive and release everyone who I mistakenly thought had injured or harmed me in any way. I forgive myself for choosing the path of the ego.

Step 6: I ask.

I ask of the Holy Spirit, with my partners as witnesses, the following: [insert personal requests].

[Response by witnesses:] I am grateful to witness your request. I support and honour what you have asked for, knowing that it will manifest in your experience.

Step 7: I accept.

I gratefully accept that the miracle-working power of the Holy Spirit has answered my request. I am joyous that I now see my situation differently.

Step 8: I make a dedication and covenant.

This covenant with the Holy Spirit supplies me with all I need for complete happiness. I am dedicated to loving God, my neighbours, and myself, and to choosing God's Will as my own. I go further in God's service with enthusiasm, excitement, and expectancy. I am at peace.

(These steps are adapted from Jack Boland's teachings on Master Mind. They offer a predictable structure for conducting a spiritual group where two or more like-minded people come together for the purpose of supporting each other and connecting with the Source.)

THE UNIVERSAL PRAYER

O Adorable Lord of Mercy and Love
Salutations and prostrations unto Thee
Thou art Omnipresent, Omnipotent, and Omniscient
Thou art Satchitananda
Thou art Existence, Knowledge, and Bliss Absolute
Thou art the Indweller of all beings.

Grant us an understanding heart, equal vision,
Balanced mind, faith, devotion, and wisdom
Grant us inner spiritual strength to resist temptation and to control the mind.
Free us from egoism, lust, anger, greed, hatred, and jealousy.
Fill our hearts with Divine Virtues.

Let us behold Thee in all these names and forms.
Let us serve Thee in all these names and forms.
Let us ever remember Thee.
Let us ever sing Thy glories.
Let Thy name be ever on our lips.
Let us abide in Thee for Ever and Ever.

— *Swami Sivananda*

WE ARE NOT ALONE IN THE UNIVERSE

"A human being is part of the whole, called by us Universe, limited in time and space. He experiences himself, his thoughts and feelings as something separated from the rest—a kind of optical delusion of his consciousness. This delusion is a prism, restricting us to our personal desires and to affection for a few persons close to us. Our task must be to free ourselves from our prism by widening our circle of compassion to embrace all humanity and the whole of nature in its beauty."

—Albert Einstein

PRAYER OF PROTECTION
(as read in the Unity Church)

The light of God surrounds us,
The love of God enfolds us,
The power of God protects us,
The presence of God watches over us,
Wherever we are, God is and all is well.

THE PRINCIPLES OF ATTITUDINAL HEALING

1. The essence of our being is Love.
2. Health is inner peace. Healing is letting go of fear.
3. Giving and receiving are the same.
4. We can let go of the past and of the future.
5. Now is the only time there is, and each instant is for giving.
6. We can learn to love ourselves and others by forgiving rather than judging.
7. We can become Love finders rather than fault finders.
8. We can choose and direct ourselves to be peaceful inside regardless of what is happening outside.
9. We are students and teachers of each other.
10. We can focus on the whole of life rather than the fragments.
11. Since Love is eternal, death need not be viewed as fearful.
12. We can always perceive others as either extending Love or giving a call for help.

—Gerald Jampolsky and the Centre for Attitudinal Healing

In our prayer room at home hangs a plaque with the following statements from *A Course in Miracles*. For years, it has been my morning ritual to visit the prayer room and read these lines before going to work.

1. I am here to be truly helpful.

2. I am here to represent Him who sent me.

3. I do not have to worry about what to say or what to do because He who sent me will direct me.

4. I am content to go wherever He wants me to go because He goes there with me.

5. I will be healed as I let Him teach me to heal.

CONCLUDING PRAYER

May we all awaken to our full potential and be liberated from the limitations and conditioning that hold us back from experiencing our unbounded and infinite nature. May all life in its various manifestations be blessed. May we co-create a Heaven on Mother Earth as we consciously awaken from the dream of illusion. May there be peace and harmony in all dimensions.

Key Insights

1. Anybody and everybody who is consciously awakening can be an usher of Heaven.

2. You are ready to awaken when you find yourself saying, "There's got to be another way to go through life rather than the status quo."

3. The silent prayer of an usher is, "May all beings be blessed."

4. To leave the world a little better place is to have succeeded as an usher.

5. An usher understands the value of service as a spiritual practice. Service softens the heart and purifies the mind for awakening.

Questions to Reflect On

1. How does it feel to reflect on your being an usher of Heaven?
2. What qualities or virtues would you like to cultivate in your personality?
3. What are some of the quotes or scriptural passages that inspire you?

Awakening Practice (Meditation for Peace)

Take a comfortable posture, either sitting on a chair or on the floor. Turn off your cell phone and make sure you won't be distracted for the next fifteen to twenty minutes. Relax, smile, and breathe mindfully for a couple of minutes, silently saying, "*I am breathing in*" as you inhale and "*I am breathing out*" as you exhale.

Now silently repeat this biblical saying: "*Peace be still and know that I am God.*" Now keep shortening this statement, until after a minute or so, "*Peace*" is the only word that you are left saying. The process of shortening the statement may look like this:

Peace be still and know that I am God.
Peace be still and know . . .
Peace be still . . .
Peace be . . .
Peace . . . Peace . . . Peace.

Now keep repeating the word "*Peace*" as a mantra for the next ten to fifteen minutes. The repetition of the mantra should be subtle like a mist rising from a lake. It is as though you are not saying the word, rather listening to it or having an idea of it. At the end of the meditation, you can just sit in silence and let peace permeate your whole being. I must acknowledge the saintly lady, "Peace Pilgrim," for introducing a similar meditation in her writings. She walked across America on foot many times in order to have a conversation with people about peace within and without.

APPENDIX A

MY TRANSFORMATIONAL CREED

- Today is a new day. I choose to live this day fully as though this is the first and the last day of my earthly life.

- I seal off past and future from the present because I know that past is nothing but dust and future is a dream yet to be born.

- I live each moment of each hour of the day with a sense of newness and being fully in the here and now.

- Today is the only day I will ever have to live.

- All things are possible today. Past does not equal future.

- I consciously create this day to be a positive, productive, happy, fulfilling, and aspiring day.

- Today I love and accept myself and others completely and unconditionally.

- I am capable, lovable, and beautiful exactly as I am. I approve of myself in all situations.

- As I go through the day and various situations, I remind myself that I can choose peace over conflict.

- I ask myself if I can be happy by blaming others and making myself right.

- I choose being happy over being right.

- Today I hold back no grievances toward myself and others.

- Today I forgive easily, knowing fully well that all forgiveness is a gift of love to me.

- Today I remember that there is nothing in this transitory world worth getting upset over. I remain established in the ultimate reality.

- Today I live like a no-limit or NEZ (no erroneous zone) person as I connect with my unbounded nature in meditations.

- Every time I experience an upset, I remind myself that the cause of my suffering is not the person or the situation but rather my conditioned self and its addictive software.

- I see all upsets as golden opportunities to reprogram the addictive software of my bio-computer.

- I uplevel all my addictive attachments and expectations to preferences.

- Today I selectively focus on what I am grateful for rather than dwelling on what is missing.

- Today I practise the art of effortless manifestation and flow through life with an experience of arriving rather than striving.

- Today I consciously connect with the Source of all life and live a life of enthusiasm and passion.

- Today I see and behold the divine presence in the whole creation. I see the divine in everybody that I encounter today.

- Today I love God the creator and serve God the creation.

- Today I remind myself that my safety lies in my defencelessness.

- Today I selectively focus on positive thoughts. I contribute only positive vibrations to the world.

- Today I do not have the luxury of any negative thoughts. I cross out all negative words from my vocabulary such as can't, have to, should, impossible, hopeless, difficult, can't afford, etc.

- I understand that I create my reality with my thinking, perception, and beliefs. What I believe is what I see.

- Today I live with faith and affirm the good even though evidence may not be there.

- Today I live as though this is the day of my Realization. I expectantly prepare for the choice hour for my Realization.

- Today I remember that for Realization I do not have to go anywhere or get anywhere because the Source is right here and now with me and all around me. I can experience it with every breath and every heartbeat.

- Today I remember my connectedness with the whole creation.
- Today I live as a spiritual being having a human experience rather than a human being striving to be spiritual.
- Today I am working toward joining and building bridges of oneness heart.
- Today I create two or more periods in the day for soulful meditations.
- Today I live my whole day in meditative consciousness as I practise mindfulness in everything I do.
- I am mindful of the chakra at which I am operating and I am consciously raising my vibration.
- Today I listen to my inner pilot and surrender my will to Thy will.
- Today I have everything that I need to live and create a truly fulfilling life because I know that my limitations are in thought only.
- Today I am free right here and right now. There are no chains that bind me.
- No person, circumstance, or situation has power over me. I am eternally free.
- Today I live in a miracle-minded consciousness.
- Today I expect and create miracles everywhere, big and small.
- Today I see my work as an opportunity full of possibilities to serve the Divine instead of clients or patients.
- Today I live prosperously and remember the source of all good.
- Today I play music and create harmony with my resources.
- Today I nurture the physical body with good nutrition, proper exercise, relaxation, and balance.
- Today I see my body as my soul's temple. I take care of this body like a temple.
- Every day in every way, I am getting healthier and healthier.
- Today I nourish my mind and soul with some positive and uplifting reading, listening, or viewing.

- Today I live with inner conviction that there is nothing that is going to happen that I and God can't handle.
- Today I know that all is well in my world now and forever, since I dwell in the ultimate reality where nothing real can be threatened and nothing unreal exists.
- Today I take the time to listen and behold the good in everybody.
- Today I see everybody as a developing soul and choose to perceive their behaviours as either loving or asking for love.
- Today I focus more on giving than on receiving.
- Today I consciously cultivate good qualities and virtues and surrender to the Supreme my imperfections for illumination.
- Today I fulfill my Lord in a special way.
- Today I live with faith and the unflickering flame of confidence, irrespective of what happens. I choose to see the good in every situation.
- Today I live a life of balance, harmony, and peace. There is ample time in my day for renewal, reflection, and just being.
- I live in rhythms with nature. I wake up early in the morning to greet the sunrise with an aspiration song.
- I conclude my day with a meditative watching of the sunset whenever possible.
- Today I function in the world like a karma yogi who focuses on the action rather than the result.
- I create this day to be joyful, loving, and aspiring.
- Today I soar like an eagle in the aspiration sky.
- Today I live the creed of a possibility thinker.
- Today I choose to learn, grow, and excel in all areas of my life.
- Today I fill my day with play, laughter, and music. Perpetual Joy is possible because that is the nature of the self.
- Today I am a success in everything I do. I radiate Divine confidence.
- Today I show unlimited capacity for creativity, problem-solving, and growth.

- Today I communicate with the world kindly and lovingly.

- I focus my energies on understanding rather than being understood.

- Today I love people and use things.

- Today I live with the knowledge that my true nature is eternal and immortal, and there is no cause for fear.

- Today I go to bed with the company of good thoughts and positive memories only. Angels and enlightened beings watch over me while I sleep.

— Sunder S. Arora (Vyasa)
February 19, 1991

MISSION STATEMENTS

Here are examples of my personal, family, and world vision statements. My personal mission statement reads more like a prayer since that format appeals to my devotional side. Our family mission statement was created through a collaborative group process. The couple mission statement was written while we were visiting the Lake Shrine temple in California during one of our winter escapes. The world vision was written after a spiritual retreat.

My Soul's Prayer

Dear Lord, mould me into an instrument of peace, joy, unconditional love, and healing. Make me a channel of creativity and Thy blessings.

May all my breaths, feelings, sensations, and thoughts be your invocation. May all my choices and actions be manifestations of your will.

May I wisely use all of my talents and resources to realize you and support my fellow beings to claim their divine right to total wellness, happiness, abundance, unconditional love, and liberation.

Be my guide and my charioteer like Krishna to Arjuna[22] when I am performing my role as a healer, communicator of truth, motivator, family member, student, physician, manager, leader, or whatever other role I may be called upon to perform.

Show me the way to be "Zorba and the Buddha" at the same time.

Teach me how to be a "psychiatrist and a *Siddha*" at the same time.

Teach me how to be a yogi while living in the world and manifesting your glories.

---

22   In the *Bhagavad-Gita*, the archer Arjuna's relationship to Lord Krishna is that of love, devotion, and surrender.

May the aspiration flame burn brighter within me with every breath.

May I always remember that You are the source of all my Good. May I never forget that You are both the Creator and the Creation.

— *Sunder S. Arora (Vyasa)*

Couple Vision

We are ever blossoming in a dynamic, ever-transcending, aspiring, loving, joyful, playful, and mutually empowering friendship and marriage with each other. We are intimate at all levels and deeply fulfilled. We are honouring and nurturing our East Indian/ Punjabi Sikh roots and Western wings of dynamism and excellence. We are in an ongoing *satsang* with each other. We are unconditionally surrendered instruments of God as we perform our roles as couple, parents, family members, friends, healers, teachers, community members, etc. We manage all our affairs and possessions prayerfully, prosperously, simply, effectively, and efficiently in a win-win manner, aligning ourselves with Divine will. We are fully established in oneness heart, peace, stillness, and radical gratitude at every moment. We dwell in a sacred sanctuary of love, light, and purity.

There is cleanliness, order, beauty, and organization in all areas of our home. Sages, saints, avatars, and enlightened beings live with us and within us in our temple of worship. We are prayerfully raising our children in a divinely confident way, loving them unconditionally, offering empathetic listening, and empowering them to reach their highest potential. We are in an honest, open, *satsang* with them, sharing our journey and our deepest truth with integrity, respect, and love. We are role models of Higher Consciousness and a divine life.

Family Mission Statement

We are a family founded upon abundant, unconditional love, respect, friendship, and righteous living. We empower each other and grow together continuously through empathic listening and honest communication, always believing in the best and highest in each other. We nurture and share our artistic, creative, and musical talents.

We are a perfect mastermind and a spiritual team that has power and energy of unlimited potential. We are friendly, forgiving, affectionate, caring, playful, and a close-knit family. We are aspiring instruments of God to bring Heaven on Earth.

We transcend our human challenges through prayer, forgiveness, and expansion of our consciousness. We embrace and nurture our East Indian, Punjabi Sikh roots and Western wings of dynamism and excellence. We celebrate our lives together in total health of body, mind, spirit, and abundance. We make a stand for dharma and integrity in all areas of our lives. The love in our hearts overflows to the whole universe and all beings.

We are a circle of loving, spiritual beings living in a human family.

World Vision

I live in a world that is a Heaven on Mother Earth and is governed by people with integrity.

I live in a world where the pervasive mood is that of peace, love, joy, and celebration. People are living their lives passionately and being fully human, fully Divine, and fully alive.

I live in a world where parents and elders are loved, respected, and honoured. Growing old is a joyful and graceful act of blossoming of consciousness.

I live in a world where all children are raised and nurtured in a way that creates geniuses like Christ, Buddha, Gandhi, and Martin Luther King. In my world, all children grow up to be responsible and enlightened citizens of the Universe.

I live in a world where the family unit is empowered and a training place to relate to the whole world as one global family.

I live in a world where the institution of marriage is honoured and celebrated.

I live in a world where everybody is consciously engaged in the pursuit of self-transcendence and awakening.

I live in a world where there is freedom, equality, and safety for all; a world where travel is safe, fun, and convenient. I live in a world without borders.

I live in a world where the environment is ecologically healthy, where rivers run clean, and all the plants, animals, and people radiate health, vitality, and the glow of life.

I live in a world where the air is fresh and the water is pure. All food is grown organically.

I live in a world where people, irrespective of their faith and creed, grow together in an atmosphere of mutual respect, understanding, and oneness consciousness.

I live in a world where radiant health and vitality is the norm. All doctors are awakening beings. The medical system is health-oriented and open to all modalities of healing.

I live in a world where I feel at home no matter where I am.

I live in a world where the best and wisest among us lead in politics and administrative positions. I live in a world where all governments co-operate and function together as a global family.

I live in a world where politicians and lawmakers take guidance and inspiration from saints and sages.

I live in a world where the educational system focuses on character and wisdom development as its primary purpose.

I live in a world where Angels, siddhas, and Ascended Masters ceaselessly shower their light and blessings upon all life on the planet.

I live in a world where even the gods line up for an opportunity to visit the Heaven on Mother Earth.

I live in a world where conflicts are seen as an opportunity for growth and are resolved through prayer, communication, forgiveness, and expansion of consciousness.

I live in a world where everybody greets each other with a smile, and neighbours look after each other and earn each other's love through altruism.

I live in a world where making transition is a joyful and sacred ritual of ascension.

I live in a world where all children are welcomed with a theme song for their earthly existence.

APPENDIX B

THE TRANSFORMATIVE JOURNALLING PROCESS

Self-reflection is a powerful tool as a daily spiritual discipline. By observing ourselves, we may appreciate the inner struggle between spirit and ego (conditioned consciousness). We all want to be free and soar, yet more often than not, we find ourselves limited by chains of habitual consciousness. Our day begins with clear resolutions, and then life happens, leaving behind a string of unfulfilled expectations. In the chapter "Dance of Two Selves," this thought is fully elaborated.

A grandfather once told his grandson about the two wolves fighting within us. One is a noble wolf (spirit) and the other, an evil wolf (ego). Grandson asks, "So which wolf wins the battle?" Grandfather replies, "The wolf you feed the most."

How to Journal

Take a blank page in your journal and divide it into four quadrants by drawing a vertical and a horizontal line.

Top right quadrant
(positive life-enhancing behaviours or ways of the spirit)

This is the quadrant where we acknowledge ourselves for all our daily activities that are in alignment with our highest intentions. Be generous and acknowledge every small personal victory; e.g., eating only half a piece of cake or doing even one sun salutation in couple of minutes instead of no yoga practice on a busy day. **Look for at least ten to twelve small victories.** Write in bullet form. Changing ourselves is like trying to grow a tree. The more you nurture it, the faster it grows.

Top left quadrant
(self-defeating behaviours or ways of the ego)

This is the quadrant where we observe our self-defeating behaviour in a milieu of non-judgmental awareness. **List no more than four behaviours in this section.**

Bottom left quadrant
(gratitude/miracles/synchronicities)

This is a section where you count your blessings; acknowledge miracles/synchronicities, big and small. Gratitude is the key to God's treasury. The more you acknowledge synchronicities and miracles, the more frequently they happen. **Aim for ten to twelve items on this list.**

Bottom right quadrant
(intentions/forgiveness/prayer)

This section is usually completed at the end of the day. The other three sections can be filled in during the day. Clarify your intentions, say or write a prayer, and, most important, forgive yourself and others.

You can do this process daily or whenever you are inspired to reflect.

I usually start my day with a fresh page and keep that page open. As I am going through the day, I make notes, which makes it lot easier to review at the end of the day. If I miss a day, simple prayers, such as "SHOW ME THE WAY," can be the most potent action in the universe.

SELF-DEFEATING BEHAVIOURS OR WAYS OF THE EGO

- Postponed exercise until evening.

- Ate snacks while watching TV.

- Checked e-mail before bedtime.

- Postponed calling a friend.

POSITIVE LIFE-ENHANCING BEHAVIOURS OR WAYS OF THE SPIRIT

- Meditated a.m. and p.m.

- Ate mindfully during lunch.

- Called family overseas.

- Loving attitude towards spouse.

- Listened to inspirational books while driving.

- Practised assertiveness with a colleague.

- Enjoyed Karaoke.

- Used priority management system.

- Communed with nature consciously.

- Renewed my driving licence.

- Got an appointment with family physician.

GRATITUDE/ MIRACLES/ SYNCHRONICITIES

- *I am grateful for..........*

- Sunny weather

- Loving connection with spouse.

- A thank you card and a gift from a client.

- The amazing Karaoke machine.

- The peaceful country that I live in.

- For the opportunity to serve.

- For the Cricket Channel.

- The family of spiritual friends.

- The blessings of technology.

- Writings of Dr David Hawkins.

- Meeting an old friend unexpectedly.

INTENTIONS/ FORGIVENESS/ PRAYER

- *May I be.........*

- Prompt in returning phone calls.

- Manage my priorities effectively

- Keep evenings for spiritual activities.

- Continue to be mindful while eating.

- Exercise earlier in the day.

- Be relaxed during the upcoming travel.

- Accepting of self and others unconditionally.

SPIRITUAL DIARY

Keeping a Spiritual Diary

"Even after following all the prescribed spiritual practices faithfully, you may run into obstructions in your efforts at meditation. In almost all cases where a seeker complains of lack of progress, it is because his subtle body has grown grosser. Do not be misled into thinking that your lack of progress is because of 'destiny' or 'a bad day' or the withdrawal of God's or your guru's grace! During an unconscious moment of relaxation, the sensuous world has invaded your inner world through the sense organs and brought forth from your subconscious mind the lower tendencies. The only way out is to gather up your strength and fight out the battle with your baser tendencies. In order to protect the growing spiritual wealth in you and not suffer the sorrow of setbacks, it may help to post twenty 'soldiers' around you, in the form of twenty questions to put to yourself at the end of each day's activities. Keep track of the questions and answers in the form of a spiritual diary that you keep strictly and continuously for three months, but never for more than six months at a stretch. You must not let yourself become habituated to diary-writing. At any time that you feel a setback in your spiritual growth, take up the diary again for a week. It is the experience of many masters and thousands of seekers that this diary-keeping is the sovereign remedy for spiritual fervor turned into sour skepticism."

— *Swami Chinmayananda*

"Blessed is he who keeps daily diary and compares the work of this week with that of the last week, for he will realize God quickly."

— *Swami Sivananda*

SPIRITUAL DIARY
(Sample)

FROM ....……… TO…………....……. 20 …........

	PERSONAL DISCIPLINES	MON	TUE	WED	THU	FRI	SAT	SUN	TOTAL
1	Wake up Time	7:30	8:00	6:40	7:00	8:00	8:30	8:30	
2	Morning Meditation	yes	—	yes	yes	—	yes	yes	5
3	Evening Meditation	yes	yes	yes	—	yes	yes	yes	6
4	Inspirational Reading	—	yes	yes	—	yes	yes	yes	5
5	Aerobic Exercise	30	40	30	45	30	40	40	7
6	Yoga/Stretching	yoga	yoga	—	—	stretch	yoga	yoga	5
7	Mindful Eating	yes	—	yes	yes	yes	yes	—	5
8	Journalling	yes	yes	—	yes	yes	—	yes	5
9	Aspiration Level (1-10)	7	6-8	7.5	8	6	7	8.5	7+
10	Bedtime	12	11	12	1 am	12	1 am	11	
11									
12									
13									
14									
15									
16									
17									
18									
19									
20									

GLOSSARY

Akhand Path. *Akhand* means uninterrupted, and *"path"* means recitation of the scriptures. Usually it takes forty-eight hours to recite the Sikh holy book, *Sri Guru Granth Sahib*.

Amritsar. *Amrit* means divine nectar, and the word *sarover* means a pond. The world-famous Golden Temple is surrounded by a body of sacred water. That is how the city of Amritsar derived its name. It is a holy city for Sikh pilgrims from all over the world.

Arjvam. The dynamic state of alignment in thinking, feeling, and action is called Arjvam. This internal alignment is the secret of worldly and spiritual success.

Asana. Yoga postures are called *asanas*. The practice of yoga prepares the mind and body for meditation.

Aurangzeb. Last in the lineage of Muslim kings who ruled India. He was known for his fanaticism and forcibly converting non-Muslims into Islam.

Ayurveda. *Ayus* means life and *Veda* means knowledge. Ayurveda is a very sophisticated, consciousness-based alternative healing system that focuses on restoring health and balance through diet, herbs, lifestyle changes, meditations, massage, etc. Dr. Deepak Chopra and his writings have popularized the 5,000-year-old science of Ayurveda in the West.

Barpunjhas. A group of people who live in a particular section of the city of Amritsar. They are usually dark-complexioned due to exposure to sun, heat, and fire. They specialize in roasting, peanuts, grahams, and rice crispies and make a variety of snack foods. Once a week, they frequently have an all-night chanting and prayer vigil (*Jagrata*).

Bhagavad-Gita. A Hindu scriptural text. The text is a dialogue between Lord Krishna and his friend and disciple Arjuna.

The dialogue occurs in the middle of a battlefield prior to the commencement of the war of Mahabharata.

Bhajans. Spiritual songs of India. Chanting God's name is a spiritual practice.

Bhakti Yoga. *Bhakti* means devotion and the word *yoga* means union; so Bhakti yoga is a devotional way to approach Divinity.

Bibi Ji. A respectful way to address a female or your mother.

Brahma Muhurta. *Brahma* means God and *muhurta* stands for an auspicious time. So in Hinduism and Sikhism, the early morning hours between four and six a.m. are considered as the divine time to practice a spiritual discipline. Even the animals in the jungle don't kill at that time.

Chi Kung. *Chi* means life force in Chinese (the Sanskrit word for it is *prana*). So Chi Kung is the discipline of managing the life force through movement, breath, and meditation.

Dadi Ji; Dada Ji. The word *dadi* in Hindi means paternal grandmother. *Dada* means paternal grandfather, and the word *ji* after a name is a sign of respect.

Dar Ji. *Dar* is an abbreviation of the word *sardar*, which means a Sikh or chief of a clan. The expression *Dar Ji* is often used in Sikh families to address the father, and Bibi Ji is for the mother.

Dharma. Righteous action that is in the greater good of the person and the universe. Each person has to discover his/her own *dharma* and therefore it requires awareness and discernment. For example, violence is universally considered not a virtuous act, yet for a surgeon, it is *dharmic* to use his knife to save a life.

Dixsha. Education that you receive from parents and elders and often not taught in the schools, as compared to *shiksha*, which is the academic information that you receive in schools. It is *shiksha* that may help you to earn a living, but to create a beautiful life, you need the wisdom of *dixsha*.

Durgyana Mandhir. *Mandhir* means "temple" in Hindi. In the city of Amritsar, there are two beautiful temples, the Golden Temple and Durgyana Mandhir.

Golden Temple. The name of a Sikh temple in Amritsar. Its domes are covered with gold plating. It is like the Mecca for Sikhs from all over the world.

Guru. One who removes darkness. "Guru Ji" is a respectful way to address one's spiritual teacher.

Gurudwara. *Dwara* means "door." A true guru is like a doorway to the ultimate reality. In everyday language, *Gurudwara* is a term for a Sikh temple.

Guru Gobind Singh. (1666–1708) The tenth and the last Sikh guru. He was a poet, saint, warrior, and a great king. He modelled how to live in the world and yet be free from it. He also created the Sikh army of Khalsas (The Pure Ones) to stand up against the unjust rule of the Muslim king Aurangzeb.

Gurukula. Simply stated, it means the family of a guru. In the olden days, people would send their young children to a *gurukula*, where they would stay with their teacher and learn, and in this way obtain both academic knowledge (*shiksha*) and wisdom (*dixsha*).

Gurumukh. One who listens to the voice of wisdom or Higher Self as compared to a *manmukh*, who is guided by the ego mind. Sikhs are encouraged to live the life of a *gurumukh*.

Guru Nanak. (1469–1539) He was the first guru and founder of the Sikh faith. His message was that of love, devotion, and surrender.

Gyana Yoga. *Gyana* means knowledge, and *yoga* stands for union with the divine. It is a path of knowledge, and the seeker is encouraged to read scriptures, contemplate, ask questions, and meditate as compared to the devotional path (Bhakti yoga) of love, devotion, and surrender.

Hatha Yoga. The branch of yoga that deals with physical postures and breathing exercises. *Ha* means sun and *tha* means moon. So this form of yoga helps to balance these sun and moon energies in the body, like the yin and yang in the Chinese system.

Hinduism. Hinduism is a term for a wide variety of related religious traditions native to India. Historically, it encompasses the development of religion in India since the Iron Age traditions, which in turn hark back to prehistoric religions such as that of Bronze Age Indus Valley civilization, followed by the Vedic religions.

Hindus. Followers of the Hindu religion. As of 2007, out of an estimated 944 million Hindus, 98.5 percent live in South Asia. Of the remaining 1.5 percent, or 14 million, 6 million live in Southeast Asia (mostly Indonesia), 2 million in Europe, 1.8 million in North America, and 1.2 million in Southern Africa.

Hour of Power. An hour-long weekly Christian inspirational program offered by the Robert Schuller ministries.

Imaginal cells. As the larva transforms into a butterfly, new cells show up in the body of the larva that seem to be imagining a different vision for the larva — hence the name imaginal cells.

Ishta Devi. *Ishta* means favourite, and *Devi* means goddess. In Hinduism, the individual can choose his favourite deity for worship, since at the level of ultimate reality there is only one God. A mother may be drawn to the image of baby Krishna, while a businessman may be inspired by Lakshmi, the goddess of prosperity.

Jagrata. *Jag* means to be awake, and *rata* means night. So *jagrata* is a term for an all-night prayer vigil.

Japa. A simple, yet powerful, spiritual practice based on remembering God's name. The aspirant may use prayer beads as an aid.

Kalidasa. A famous Sanskrit poet born in the fourth or fifth century CE. According to the story, there lived a princess who was very intelligent and could not be defeated in a debate by any of the intellectuals in the king's court. Her condition was that she would only marry someone who could defeat her in a public debate. So the scholars in the kingdom decided to look for a fool to teach the proud and arrogant princess a lesson. They found somebody so foolish that he was cutting the branch that he was sitting on. A nonverbal debate was arranged. The princess showed a hand with five fingers and the fool thought that she intended to slap him and he gestured with a fist. The panel of scholars ascribed a symbolic meaning to the gestures and declared him the winner. On the honeymoon night, the princess discovered that he was in fact a fool and that she had been deceived. She asked him to leave and only return when he was educated. Several years later, he returned back to her as Kalidasa, the great Sanskrit scholar.

Karma. Any thought, word, or deed is considered as karma. The law of karma is as precise as the law of gravity. Whatever seeds of karma you sow, you will reap the harvest in this lifetime or the next one. Spiritual practice, meditation, and grace can fry the seeds of karma and prevent them from germinating.

Karma yoga. People who are very action-oriented are encouraged to bring God consciousness in their working life. Every action is performed as an act of worship without any attachment to the fruits of the action. The result is accepted as a Divine blessing.

Kaurvas. In the epic of Mahabharata, there was described a great war between two clans: the Kaurvas, representing the forces of darkness and ego, and the Pandvas, representing the forces of light and higher consciousness. Lord Krishna favoured the forces of light, and they were ultimately victorious after eighteen days of fierce fighting.

Koan. In Zen Buddhism, the spiritual aspirant is usually given a question (*koan*) to solve. The questions are impossible to answer with the intellect, therefore it forces the seeker to transcend the mind and enter into the domain of being. Some examples of the *koan* are: "What was your face like before your father was born?" and "What is the sound of one hand clapping?"

Kshma Parmo dharma. *Kshma* means forgiveness. *Parmo* means supreme and *dharma* is the Sanskrit word for a righteous act. Forgiveness is the most perfect action in this imperfect world.

Mahabharata. The Hindu epic of Mahabharata describes a great war between two clans. The Kaurvas represented the forces of darkness and ego and the Pandvas represented the forces of light and Higher Consciousness.

Maharaj Ji. *Maha* means great and *raja* means king. The title Maharaj Ji is used to address either a great king or a spiritual master. We addressed our family guru as Maharaj Ji.

Mandala. A sacred geometric pattern, usually a circle, used as an aid in meditation rituals in the Hindu and Buddhist traditions. A mandala can also be created with coloured sand, a favourite technique of Tibetan Buddhist lamas.

Manmukh. *Man* means mind and *mukh* means face. This is an expression reserved for a man living a life directed by the egocentric mind, compared to a Gurumukh, who lives his life directed by the Higher Self.

Metta. *Metta* is a Pali word for loving kindness. The Buddha taught a very heart-opening meditation some 2,500 years ago. It has found its way into mainstream consciousness as the *metta* meditation or loving-kindness meditation.

Nanak dhukhia sab sansar. This is a poetic statement from the Sikh scriptures. It describes the unsatisfactory nature of life where everybody sooner or later suffers from some malady, physical or emotional.

Nirvana. Nirvana means the end of suffering. In the Pali language, the word "*nibbana*" means blowing out the fires of greed, hatred, and delusion. The word is a central concept in Buddhism and Jainism. The Christian equivalent of this word is "salvation." The Hindu expression for this state of freedom from suffering would be "enlightenment."

Om. *Om* is considered the primordial sound of creation. The sound has a similar vibration to the word "Amen" in Christianity and "Ameen" in Islam. Merely chanting this sound can raise the vibration of the chanter and those around him or her. NASA has recorded our sun making a similar vibrational sound. The sound has a very healing and nurturing influence on healthy cells and an opposite effect on cancer cells.

Om Namah Shivaya. This is a famous Hindu mantra often chanted during worship rituals or as an aid to meditation. A very simplistic translation would be, "I bow to the Divine."

Pandvas. In the Hindu epic of Mahabharata, the Pandvas were fighting for truth and righteousness and therefore were favoured by the Lord Krishna.

Pavlovian dogs. The term is coined after a Russian scientist, Ivan

Pavlov, who did experiments of classical conditioning on dogs. Pavlov used a metronome to call the dogs to their food, and after a few repetitions, the dogs started to salivate in response to the metronome.

Puja. A ritual of worship in Hinduism. It is also sometimes spelled *pooja*. Most Hindus would have a *puja* altar in their homes, with pictures and idols of their chosen deities.

Punjab. A state in Northwest India with five rivers. It is a rich agricultural land and considered to be the breadbasket of India.

Pranayama. *Prana* means life force and *yama* means control. *Pranayama* involves a series of breathing exercises designed to build an energy reserve in the body. It is an integral part of yoga practice and self-care.

Prasad. Something usually edible that is first offered to a deity during a worship ritual and then consumed. It is considered sacred and a Divine blessing.

Raja yoga. Literally, "royal yoga." It is an elaborate eightfold path of yoga systematically designed to take the seeker to the highest level of spiritual unfoldment. It seems to appeal to people with a scientific and/or mystical temperament. The practice involves a foundation of ethical living and physical self-care through yoga postures and *pranayama* followed by practising different concentration and meditation exercises.

Ramayana. One of the two great epics of India, the other being the Mahabharata. It offers role models of relationships like the ideal brother, the ideal wife, the ideal husband, and the ideal king.

Sadhana. A discipline undertaken in the pursuit of a goal. It is often used to describe a spiritual practice or a process-oriented activity such as music.

Sadhu. In Hinduism, *sadhu* is a common term for an ascetic or a wandering monk.

Samaskaras. *Sanskar* is a variant of the Sanskrit word *samaskaras* and signifies cultural heritage and upbringing in modern Hindi.

Sangha. In Sanskrit or Pali, it is a spiritual community.

Sant. Often a prefix used to describe a saintly person.

Saraswati. In Hinduism, Saraswati is the goddess of music, wisdom, and the arts. She is also the mother of the Vedas.

Sardar. Sikh men are also addressed as Sardar Ji and Sikh women as Sardarni Ji. Literally translated, *sardar* means a chief or a head of a clan. Sikh men who wear the traditional turban do stand out in the crowd.

Saree. Also spelled *sari*, the *saree* is an unstitched cloth ranging from four to nine metres in length that is draped over the body in various styles. It is very popular in India, Bangladesh, Nepal, Pakistan, Sri Lanka, Bhutan, Burma, and Malaysia.

Sarvam Dhukham. *Sarvam* means everybody and *dhukham* means suffering. It is a Sanskrit aphorism to describe the unsatisfactory nature of life. It is not meant to be a fatalistic statement but rather a realistic diagnosis of the condition of life before a remedy is offered.

Sat Chit Ananda. A compound Sanskrit word: *sat* (truth), *chit* (consciousness), and *ananda* (bliss); it describes the state of Divinity or a liberated yogi.

Sat naam Wahe Guru. A mantra from the Sikh tradition that is often chanted or silently repeated. It refers to the Supreme Being, whose name is truth and who is the most wonderful teacher.

Satsang. *Sat* means truth and *sangha* means company in Sanskrit. Satsang means company of truth. When spiritual seekers come together to meditate and share their spiritual journey or listen to a visiting guru, it is a *satsang*.

Sattva. The quality of purity, goodness, and subtlety.

Sesshin. A period of intense meditation practice (zazen) in a Zen monastery. In the West, many Zen teachers offer a week-long *sesshin* to the students of their Zen school.

Shakti. The ever-free primordial energy of transformation, often worshipped in a feminine form. In Hinduism, Shakti is referred to as the great Divine mother.

Shanti. It means peace. Usually at the end of Vedic chanting, the Shanti mantra is repeated: *Om Shanti, Shanti, Shanti.*

Shivoham. Shiva is the Hindu term for the creator. Shivoham is a Sanskrit mantra and a reminder that we, too, are Divine, since like a wave in the ocean we share oneness with the creator.

Shwetasvatra Upanishad. Upanishads are those Hindu scriptures that contain the core teachings of Vedanta. There are 108 Upanishads and Shwetasvatra is one of the scriptures named after a sage.

Soham. A Sanskrit mantra meaning "I myself" or "It is I." It is a mantra often used in meditations. When it applies to a person's name, according to Vedic philosophy it means identifying oneself with the universe or ultimate reality. Some say that when a child is born, it cries, "Koham-Koham," which means, "Who am I?" That is when the universe replies back, "Soham. You are the same as I am." It also stems from the Sanskrit word that means "self-pride."

Tai Chi. An internal Chinese martial art often practised for health and well-being.

Turban. An English word loosely used to refer to several forms of headgears.

Vyasa. Vyasa is also referred to as Veda Vyasa. He is the central and revered figure in the Hindu tradition. He is accredited as the scribe of the Vedas, the ancient texts.

Yagna. In Hinduism, a ritual of worship aimed at pleasing the gods. An essential element of the *yagna* is *Agni* (sacred fire).

BIBLIOGRAPHY OF TRANSFORMATIVE BOOKS

Here is a short list of some of the contemporary books that I found helpful in my spiritual journey. What was actually transformative in these books was not from merely reading them once but from consciously assimilating the wisdom through repeated reading or listening and applying it in my day-to-day life. As somebody said so wisely, it may take a month to read a book but it can take a lifetime to embody the wisdom contained in the book.

Bays, Brandon. *The Journey: A Practical Guide to Healing Your Life and Setting Yourself Free.* London, England: Thorsons, 1999.

Caddy, Eileen. *Opening Doors Within.* Forres, Scotland: Findhorn Press, 1987.

Casey, Karen. *Daily Meditations for Practicing the Course.* Center city, MN: Hazelden, 1995.

Chinmayananda, Swami. *Commentary on Bhagvad Gita.* Mumbai, India: Thompson Press, 2006.

Chinmoy, Sri. *Meditation: Man-Perfection in God-Satisfaction.* Jamaica, NY: Agni Press, 1978.

———. *My Life's Soul Journey: Daily Meditations for Ever Increasing Spiritual Fulfillment.* Jamaica, NY: Aum Publications, 1995.

Chopra, Deepak. *How to Know God: The Soul's Journey into the Mystery of Mysteries.* New York: Random House, Inc., 2000.

———. *Perfect Health: The Complete Mind Body Guide.* New York: Three River Press, 1991.

A Course in Miracles. Tiburon, CA: Foundation for Inner Peace, 1976.

Covey, Stephen R. *The 7 Habits of Highly Effective People: Powerful Lessons in Personal Change.* New York: Simon & Schuster, 1989.

Dyer, Wayne. *The Power of Intention.* Carlsbad, CA: Hay House, Inc., 2004.

Hanh, Thich Nhat. *The Miracle of Mindfulness.* Boston: Beacon Press, 1999.

———. *You Are Here.* Boston: Shambhala, 2009.

Hay, Louise. *You Can Heal Your Life.* Carlsbad, CA: Hay House, Inc., 1984.

Hicks, Esther, and Jerry Hicks. *Ask and It Is Given.* Vancouver: Hay House, Inc., 2004.

Hill, Napoleon. *The Master Key to Riches.* New York: Ballantine Books, 1965.

Jones, Laurie Beth. *The Path: Creating Your Mission Statement for Work & Life.* New York: Hyperion Books, 1998.

Kabat-Zin, Jon. *Wherever You Go, There You Are: Mindfulness Meditation in Everyday Life.* New York: Hyperion Books, 1994.

Lawrence, Brother. *The Practice of the Presence of God with Spiritual Maxims.* Grand Rapids, MI: Spire Books, 1958.

Satir, Virginia et al. *The Satir Model: Family Therapy and Beyond.* Palo Alto, CA: Science and Behavior Books, 1991.

Subramuniyam, Satguru Sivaya. *Merging with Siva.* USA, Himalayan Academy, 1999.

Tolle, Eckhart. *The Power of Now: A Guide to Spiritual Enlightenment.* Vancouver: Namaste Publishing, 2004.

Yogananda, Paramahansa. *An Autobiography of a Yogi.* Nevada City, CA: Crystal Clarity Pub., 1993.

ABOUT THE AUTHOR

Sunder S. Arora (Vyasa), M.D., is an adult and child psychiatrist, an interfaith minister, yoga teacher, family man, and inspiring spiritual teacher.

In this book, he combines the wisdom of yoga, metaphysics, quantum physics, psychology, and practical wisdom gleaned from over thirty years of clinical experience and a personal spiritual quest.

He creates a bridge between east and west, science and spirituality, worldly life and mystical realms.

He strives to fulfill his soul's mission of experiencing Heaven within and manifesting it in the world. He aspires to be fully human, fully Divine, and fully alive.

He cherishes his Indian roots of spirituality and his Western wings of dynamism. He was ordained as an interfaith minister by Rabbi Joseph H. Gelberman of All Faith Seminary International, New York.

Vyasa is his spiritual name, bestowed on him lovingly by Swami Vishnudevananda, the disciple of Swami Sivananda of Rishikesh, India.

He offers his work with love and gratitude to his human family.

TO ORDER MORE COPIES:

GENERAL STORE PUBLISHING HOUSE

499 O'Brien Road, Box 415, Renfrew, Ontario, Canada K7V 4A6
Tel 1.800.465.6072 • Fax 1.613.432.7184
www.gsph.com